MERMAID WISDOM

***

MERMAID WISDOM

* * *

ENRICH YOUR LIFE WITH
INSIGHTS FROM THE DEEP

Brenda Rosen

A GODSFIELD BOOK
www.godsfield.co.uk

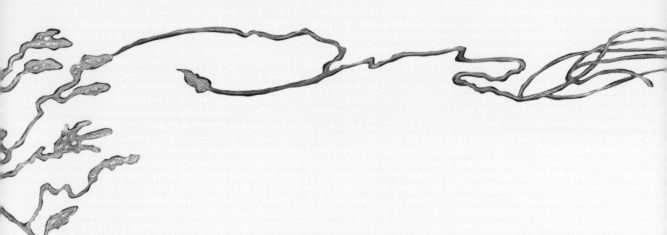

For Joe and David

First published in Great Britain in 2006 by Godsfield Press,
a division of Octopus Publishing Group Ltd
2–4 Heron Quays, London E14 4JP

Copyright © Octopus Publishing Group 2006

Distributed in the United States and Canada by
Sterling Publishing Co., Inc.
387 Park Avenue South, New York, NY 10016-8810

A CIP catalogue record for this book is available from the British Library

ISBN-13: 978-1-84181-311-0
ISBN-10: 1-84181-311-7

1 3 5 7 9 10 8 6 4 2

Printed and bound in China

CONTENTS

Introduction

* * *

For most of the world's history, people have believed that mermaids really exist. Early naturalists included mermaids among the creatures of the deep. Sea travellers and sailors reported frequent mermaid sightings and encounters. Well into the nineteenth century crowds gathered to see mermaids that had been captured alive or stuffed for display.

Even more interesting is the role that mermaids have played in human imagination. From Classical epics to folktales and popular legends, from paintings, carvings and sculptures to poetry, music and novels, mermaids have featured in the mythology and culture of people all over the world from the earliest times to the present day.

What is it about the mermaid that has made her so lastingly popular and so significant? And why should you be interested in exploring mermaid stories and pondering mermaid wisdom?

To answer these questions, you must first lay aside the popular conception of the mermaid as the sweet and spirited undersea heroine of a happily-ever-after fairy tale. In stories from every culture the mermaid is a powerful feminine presence, not a lovesick little girl. In her original Classical form she is a sea goddess, an aspect of the Great Mother connected to the sea of birth and creativity and worshipped at seaside temples that ringed the Mediterranean. In folk beliefs and legends she is a female force to be reckoned with – a semi-divine being who can be both beneficent and wrathful. Mermaids, you will find, can calm storms at sea and assure fishermen of a good catch, as well as sink ships and drag sailors down to a watery grave.

This book explores the history and meaning of the mermaid in three ways: through retellings of mermaid tales from around the world; through discussions of the mermaid as a mythological, psychological and spiritual symbol; and through practical exercises and rituals that help you tap into the wisdom of the mermaid and use it to enrich your own life.

Mermaid Tales

The mermaid tales in this book come from many lands. As you will discover, mermaids are found not only in the world's oceans, but also in lakes, rivers, fountains and wells – anywhere there is water. They take different forms, depending on where a story originates. In cold, northern cultures mermaids sometimes wear a sealskin rather than a fishtail. In the South Seas they wear coral and pearls. Some are easily able to trade their fishtails for human legs; others walk on land only with great emotional or physical pain. A few find happiness with human partners, though for most mermaids marriage to a

mortal is problematic. In other words, the lives of mermaids are as various and as interesting as human lives. Whatever your circumstances, you are sure to find a mermaid in this book whose story resonates with yours.

Mermaid Insights

Mermaid mythology takes you back to the earliest accounts of creation, to attempts by various cultures to explain the origins of life on Earth. Fish are an ancient symbol of fertility and, as a form of the Great Mother, the mermaid is linked to the waters of the womb, the generative sea from which all human life is born. Like all mythological goddesses, the mermaid is also an important feminine archetype, a symbol of the recurring cycle of birth, death and rebirth. Just as life comes from the sea, in many world mythologies, so death is a return to the sea's embrace. Stories that link the mermaid to shipwrecks and death by drowning may have arisen from this early mythological source.

From these noble beginnings, the mermaid was cited as an example of lust by the Church in the Middle Ages as part of its moralizing against women and against sexuality. The current surge of interest in the mermaid may signal that it is time to rescue her from both denunciation as a seductress and trivialization as a cartoon-like creature, who is willing to do anything to gain a soul or win a man's love.

Psychologically, the mermaid's power derives from her connection to the world's waters. Throughout history the sea has represented the unknown and the unexplored. Ancient maps often pictured mermaids in uncharted waters, perhaps as a warning to sailors of the dangers of venturing too far from home. Today, depth psychologists (psychologists of the unconscious mind, generally followers of Carl Jung) regard the sea as a symbol of the unconscious – the unknown, and sometimes unexplored, part of your own mind. As you will discover, diving into the waters of the unconscious

is perhaps the most important way of learning about yourself.

As a spiritual symbol, it's important to keep in mind that although ancient cultures worshipped the mermaid as a goddess, for most people today she is not a supernatural helper, like a saint, angel or fairy. Rather, she is most helpful spiritually as a representative of the Divine Feminine: God in female form. Whatever your spiritual beliefs, you will find that honouring the mermaid as an empowering aspect of the world's imagination and spirit can help you deepen your connection to the most sacred part of yourself.

Exercises and Rituals

The exercises in this book give you the opportunity to experience all aspects of the mermaid. As you read the mermaid myths and folktales and work through the exercises based on them, you will learn techniques that you can use to work with the symbols in any myth or story so that it becomes a guide to personal growth and transformation.

You will discover how the mermaid can help you find your own forms of creative expression. You will be inspired by the mermaid to set aside private time for inner work such as journaling and meditation. You will let the mermaid connect you to the wild and natural woman inside you and help you love and appreciate your own unique style of beauty. You will learn from the mermaid's example how to improve your relationships and use your sexuality wisely. You will gain insight into ways of balancing and harmonizing the various aspects of your complex life. And, perhaps most important, you will learn how working with the archetypes that appear in myths, imagination and dreams can give you access to the deepest parts of yourself.

As you will see, mermaids are alluring and sensuous, independent and courageous, self-assured and heroic. They are as complex and various as human women, often helpful but sometimes harmful. Everyone who honours femininity as intelligent and spiritual, as well as sexual and beautiful, will find the mermaid an inspiring role model.

CHAPTER 1
THE FIRST MERMAIDS

***

Since once I sat upon a promontory

And heard a mermaid, on a dolphin's back,

Uttering such dulcet and harmonious breath

That the rude sea grew civil at her song,

And certain stars shot madly from their spheres

To hear the sea-maid's music.

WILLIAM SHAKESPEARE (1564–1616),
A MIDSUMMER NIGHT'S DREAM

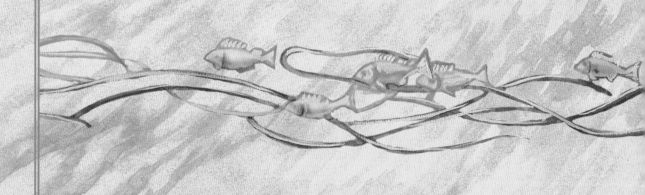

The mermaid riding on a dolphin's back that Oberon, King of the Fairies, describes in Shakespeare's *A Midsummer Night's Dream* is no cartoon princess. Her song can calm storms and charm stars to shoot from their orbits. A sister to Aphrodite, the Greek goddess of love, she is an image of feminine power, courage, creativity and self-confidence, who has been a central figure in myth and legend in nearly every culture since earliest times.

Where, you might be wondering, did the mermaid come from? Why have people all over the world told stories about her? And what does she have to do with me?

To answer these questions, this chapter begins with a reconstruction of the myth of Atargatis, the earliest mermaid story we know of. It embodies many of the themes that will be explored in this book: the connections between the mermaid and the goddess, the dangers of beauty, and the sea as a symbol of freedom and transformation. You will also read the story of the sea nymph Galatea from Ovid's *Metamorphoses*. It introduces another important mermaid theme: the perils and difficulties of love between species – mermaids and mortals, women and men! You will also gain experience in basic techniques for working with myths and archetypes, and will begin to explore the connections between the mermaid and your own life and concerns.

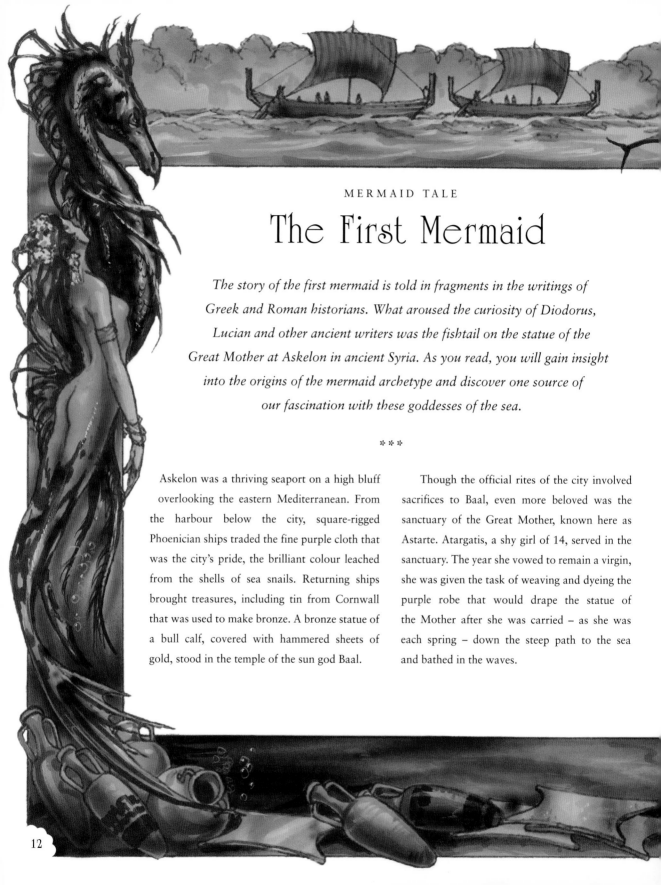

The First Mermaid

The story of the first mermaid is told in fragments in the writings of Greek and Roman historians. What aroused the curiosity of Diodorus, Lucian and other ancient writers was the fishtail on the statue of the Great Mother at Askelon in ancient Syria. As you read, you will gain insight into the origins of the mermaid archetype and discover one source of our fascination with these goddesses of the sea.

* * *

Askelon was a thriving seaport on a high bluff overlooking the eastern Mediterranean. From the harbour below the city, square-rigged Phoenician ships traded the fine purple cloth that was the city's pride, the brilliant colour leached from the shells of sea snails. Returning ships brought treasures, including tin from Cornwall that was used to make bronze. A bronze statue of a bull calf, covered with hammered sheets of gold, stood in the temple of the sun god Baal.

Though the official rites of the city involved sacrifices to Baal, even more beloved was the sanctuary of the Great Mother, known here as Astarte. Atargatis, a shy girl of 14, served in the sanctuary. The year she vowed to remain a virgin, she was given the task of weaving and dyeing the purple robe that would drape the statue of the Mother after she was carried – as she was each spring – down the steep path to the sea and bathed in the waves.

Loving solitude, Atargatis liked to wander along the bluffs with her bow and arrow. One spring morning she laid the just-washed robe to dry on a sunny promontory. As she drowsed nearby, she was startled awake by a male voice. 'What's this?' the voice said gruffly. 'The goddess of these shores, or I'm dreaming. See, there's the purple dress I've heard tell of in seamen's tales. Sure this is the reward I've dreamed of all these months upon the sea.'

Atargatis sprang to her feet and sprinted away, clutching the purple robe to her breast. But the sailor's feet were swift, and soon he threw her to the ground, crushing the purple robe beneath her. No one heard Atargatis' cries – and no one heard the death cry of the sailor as the arrow from her bow caught him smartly between the shoulder blades as he strolled away.

In time Atargatis' swollen belly told her woe. When her pains began, she fled to the bluffs and there gave birth to a daughter. Laying the babe in a nest of soft grasses, she spread her arms wide and jumped from the cliff, hurtling headlong towards the sea.

A fisherman hauling in his nets on the shore found them suddenly heavy. Amidst the wriggling hoard lay a creature such as no one had ever seen: from the waist up, a woman; but below a fish, with a tail of silver and pearl.

A priestess explained it: 'The Great Mother has washed away Atargatis' grief and shame. She is become a goddess of the deep.' From that day, Astarte herself sported a fishtail, and fish were called sacred and were never eaten.

And the babe? It is said she was fostered by doves, sacred to the Mother, and grew up to become Semiramis, fabled Queen of Babylon, who built its wondrous Hanging Gardens.

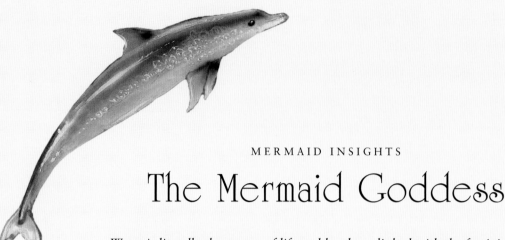

The Mermaid Goddess

Water is literally the source of life and has been linked with the feminine since time out of mind. In cultures the world over, the ocean is the womb of creation, and Mother goddesses come from the waters.

✳ ✳ ✳

In Egypt, Isis is goddess of the serpents of the primeval waters and brings the annual life-giving Nile flood. In Australia, the Rainbow Serpent, the Aboriginal creative spirit of the Dreamtime, lives in water holes and brings rain and thunder. In Genesis, life begins when the Holy Spirit broods like a mother bird over the abyss. In the New Testament, Mary's name comes from the Latin *mare*, which means 'the sea'. Mermaids, brightly painted on the prows of sailing ships and celebrated in art and legend, are probably a popular version of this ancient goddess tradition.

The first mermaid in a form you would recognize probably came from ancient Syria, as you have read (see pages 12–13). Seaside temples to Atargatis, the mermaid goddess, are known to have existed throughout the Mediterranean world.

The Greek historian Lucian, writing in the second century BCE, says that in Atargatis' temple at Hierapolis (now in modern Turkey) her fishtailed statue was decorated with jewels, and the fish in her sacred ponds wore gems in their fins, lips and gills. In Greece she is called Derketo, and her shrine on the island of Delos was surrounded by fish-filled pools and trees full of doves.

Over time, Atargatis became entwined with other Mother goddesses, the most important of which is the Greek goddess of love, Aphrodite. In a Greek creation myth, Aphrodite's father is Ouranos (Heaven), whose son Chronos (Time) 'harvests' his father's genitals and tosses them into the sea to create a space for life between Heaven and Earth (his wife Gaia).

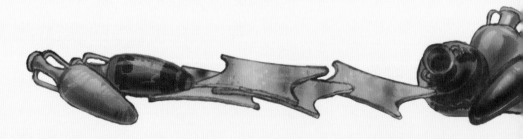

Aphrodite, born from the resulting sea foam, skims across the waves riding on the backs of dolphins. Or she wafts to shore on a half-scallop shell, as in the famous painting *The Birth of Venus* (c. 1485) by Renaissance master Sandro Botticelli. When Aphrodite steps out of the waves onto dry land, flowers spring up under her feet and animals are filled with longing for each other. Like the mermaids you will read about, Aphrodite reminds you that you come alive when you joyfully remember that the animal part of you, including your sexual nature, is lovely and holy.

All of the great goddesses invite you to experience your wholeness. A statue of Demeter, another important Greek Mother goddess, shows her holding a fish in one hand and a dove in the other – sacred animals of Atargatis and Aphrodite. The fish represents your physical body linked to the sea as the womb of life. The dove is your soul, the part that connects you to the Divine. The unmistakable message of the mermaid goddess is: love every part of who you are.

The Sea Nymphs

* * *

Like other early maritime people, the Greeks populated the sea with fantastic creatures. The poet Hesiod (c. 700 BCE) says that the union of Oceanus (the earth-encircling river) and Tethys (the fertile ocean) filled the sea with three thousand daughters, whose task it was to look after the depths.

One of these daughters was Doris, known for her sea-grey eyes and lovely hair. Doris and Nereus, an ancient sea god often called 'the old man of the sea', were parents of the Nereids or sea nymphs. These beautiful young women, 50 in number, rode through the waves on seahorses wearing seashells in their hair. Though they lacked fishtails, it's not hard to see their connection to mermaids. By the time of Pliny the Elder, who included mermaids in his *Natural History* (80 CE), Nereids and mermaids had become synonymous.

Behind these myths are traditions related to the livelihood and safety of people whose life depends on the sea. Doris was probably the goddess of the rich fishing grounds at the mouth of rivers, where fresh water mingles with brine. The Nereids may recall a group of 50 moon-priestesses whose rites ensured a bountiful catch. Nereids could also foretell the future, a gift that became associated with mermaids. Always friendly and protective towards sailors, they warned of perilous storms.

Perhaps the best-known Nereid is Galatea. She is reminiscent of Aphrodite and other mermaid goddesses as she rides laughing across the waves in a scallop-shell chariot drawn by dolphins in the fresco *The Triumph of Galatea* by Raphael (c. 1513). Encircling Galatea, sea gods blow seashell trumpets, winged cupids aim love arrows, and lusty fishtailed mermen embrace beautiful naked sea nymphs.

The Sea Nymph and the Cyclops

Galatea's story of the transforming power of love is told in Metamorphoses
*(8 BCE) by the Roman poet Ovid, based on a Greek myth. Like the story of
Atargatis, it ends with a mortal becoming a water deity.*

* * *

Polythemus, a Cyclops, an ugly one-eyed giant, lived all alone on an island, except for his sheep. One day, gazing out to sea, he spied the lovely sea nymph Galatea splashing in the waves and fell instantly in love.

Love changed the monster. Using a pool for a mirror, he combed his shaggy hair and used a sickle to trim his beard. He wooed Galatea with love songs. 'I too, claim the sea as a parent,' he sang. 'Marry me and the supreme sea god Poseidon will be your father-in-law.'

But Galatea loved another – the downy-cheeked mortal Acis. While Polythemus serenaded her, Galatea was embracing Acis behind a rock. When he discovered the pair, Polythemus' angry roar caused Mount Etna to tremble.

Galatea dived into the ocean to escape, but Acis – no sea creature – could only run. The giant broke off a piece of mountain and heaved it at the youth, crushing him instantly.

Later Galatea crept from the sea to mourn. As she wept, blood began to trickle from the rock that covered Acis. The earth split open, and through the cleft melting snow and spring rains turned the trickle to a mighty river. Waist-deep in the torrent stood Acis, transformed into a blue-green river god.

The Waters of Life and Death

Even in ancient times the mermaid was regarded as beautiful, but dangerous – a sea enchantress likely to lure unsuspecting sailors to a watery grave. Given her ties to the Mother goddess and to peaceful sea nymphs like Galatea, you might wonder how the mermaid got such a bad reputation?

* * *

The simplest explanation is that picturing mermaids as a threat to sailors was effective propaganda. Merchant sailors and colonizers had a vested interest in cautioning competitors to steer clear of their trade routes. On early maps, mermaids were often drawn in unknown waters along with sea monsters and other perils. Tales of predatory mermaids warned explorers and commercial rivals to stay in familiar territory.

But a deeper and more interesting answer lies in the mermaid's connection to the Great Mother. Cultures that honoured the feminine knew that the same goddess who gives life also takes it away. If you are born from your mother the sea, death is a return to her embrace.

The Feminine Serpent

As the divinity of life and death, the goddess is imaged as a snake as well as a fish. In the Sumerian creation myth, the Mother goddess Nammu is both the sea and a great serpent that gives birth to Heaven and Earth. When the Sumerian culture gives way to the Babylonian, Nammu becomes the bloated sea dragon Tiamat in the Babylonian epic of creation. Tiamat is defeated by the hero Marduk – a sky, wind and sun god – who splits her open like a shellfish to create the Earth and the sky.

Serpent goddesses like Nammu and Tiamat are grandmothers to the mermaid. Early woodcuts and drawings sometimes picture the mermaid as half-woman, half-snake, with a long coiling, sinuous

tail. A statue of Atargatis discovered at her temple in Rome shows the mermaid goddess encircled by a serpent that coils around her body seven times. The face of the goddess emerges from the serpent's mouth to make it clear that the two are one.

In goddess cultures, serpents were seen as benevolent and as intimately connected to the feminine principle. The snake's coiling path symbolizes the spiral of life and death. When you enter this world, an umbilical cord twisted like two snakes connects you to your mother; when you leave it, it was hoped, you shed your old skin like a snake and are reborn to new life. But in cultures in which male sky gods prevailed, the feminine serpent became a tempter and a bringer of death. In the central image in Michelangelo's Sistine Chapel ceiling (1509–1512), a mermaid-like creature with a female body from the waist up and with a snake or fish body from the waist down tempts Adam and Eve to eat the apple, the punishment for which is banishment and death.

The shift from Nammu, the life-giving mother, to Tiamat, the death-dealing sea dragon, prefigures what happened to the mermaid. When cultures turned away from veneration of the feminine divinities of the seas towards the worship of the male gods of sun and sky, the reputation of the mermaid suffered.

Yet today's interest in the mermaid signals that the time may have come to rehabilitate her and reclaim her as a guide to renewal and transformation.

Work with Myths

Myth is the DNA of the human spirit. Though the mermaid myths you will read in this book may at first seem far removed from your everyday experiences, working with them can help you to see more clearly who you are now, and step more confidently into the person you wish to become.

Long ago mermaid goddesses were objects of worship – personifications of the forces of nature and supernatural helpers believed to have the power to calm storms at sea and ensure a bountiful day's fishing. Today it is far more useful to see mermaids and other mythological beings as glorious images of feminine possibility: characters from the world's story that can teach you by example how to better appreciate your own complexity, courage, creativity, resilience and passion.

The understanding that myth can be a guide to personal growth and transformation began in earnest with the work of Swiss psychiatrist Carl Jung (1875–1961). Jung and the depth psychologists (see page 8) who followed him believed that each human mind contains a vast reservoir of universal images, which Jung called 'archetypes'. An archetype is a psychological idea or pattern that all human beings have in common. It can be a character or a relationship, such as the wise old man or the bond between mother and child; a symbol, such as a circle or spiral; a place, such as an island or a fresh-water spring; a story event or pattern, such as a marriage or heroic quest. Archetypes are the building blocks of myth, and you will find that they also appear in your dreams and creative imagination.

The existence of archetypes helps to explain why the sea has always been identified with the feminine. Since every human life begins in the briny waters of a mother's womb, it makes sense that people everywhere connect the sea and the mother. Likewise, since fish have long been regarded as symbols of fertility, the half-fish, half-woman mermaid is an ideal archetype for the mysterious generative power of the feminine, which can create life as abundantly as the sea.

The exercises in this book are aimed at helping you work creatively with the mermaid archetype. Along the way you will be encouraged to look closely at your memories, dreams and creative imaginings. Often you will use myths and stories as jumping-off points for your explorations. Working with myths can help you to recognize the universal dimension of your experiences and to step back and put your own experiences in perspective. If you let her, the mermaid can be your guide to a deeper appreciation of your own feminine power and mystery.

Picture your Mermaid Self

Each archetype expresses itself in many ways. Picturing your mermaid self helps you understand how the mermaid archetype is manifesting in your life right now. As you'll discover, your mermaid self may reflect hidden aspects of your personality.

* * *

HERE'S WHAT TO DO

1 **Take some time** to write about, draw, paint, make a collage or describe in some other concrete way yourself as a mermaid.

- What do you look like?
- How do you act?
- In what setting do you feel most at home?

2 **Your understanding** of your mermaid self will deepen as you read the stories and do the exercises that follow. Put your picture of your mermaid self in a safe place so that you can use it for an exercise later in the book (see pages 50–51).

Enter into a Myth

Mermaid tales are entertaining to read and interesting to think about, but to appreciate their full benefit you need to go beyond simply enjoying and ruminating on the stories you read in this book. Myth is powerful because it captures universal human experiences. When you enter into a myth and its archetypes using your creative imagination and your emotions, you gain valuable insights into your own life story.

In this exercise you will enter into the archetypes in the myth of Atargatis (see pages 12–13). As you do so, you will learn a basic technique for using any myth or story to increase your self-knowledge. For this exercise (and others in this book) you will gain most if you set aside time alone to experience the exercise fully. You will find it useful to keep a journal or notebook in which you can write about your experiences and record your insights.

* * *

HERE'S WHAT TO DO

1 **Sit comfortably,** close your eyes and take several deep breaths, focusing your attention on the rise and fall of your abdomen as you breathe. With each breath, release any tension in your body and allow yourself to relax more deeply.

2 **Let a picture arise in your mind** of an ancient sea coast, perhaps on the Mediterranean. Use all your inner senses to bring the scene vividly to life in your mind. Smell the salty breeze; listen to the waves lapping against the rocks and to the cries of the sea birds; see brightly painted fishing boats bobbing at anchor.

3 **Now imagine in this picture** a Greek-style temple, with graceful marble pillars. Inside this temple is a fishtailed statue of the Mother goddess. A young woman dressed in flowing white is playing an instrument and singing softly. An older woman with greying hair, her face shining in the light of a flickering torch, is telling a story to a group of younger women gathered around her. Another woman is arranging flowers near the statue of the mermaid goddess.

4 **Picture yourself in this scene,** using your creative imagination to play each role in turn:
• Imagine that you are walking along the sea coast towards the temple. What does the sea symbolize for you?

- Visualize yourself as the temple singer. Is your song happy or sad? What are some of the words of the song you are singing?
- Imagine that you are the grey-haired priestess telling the story. What are some of the words of the story you are narrating?
- Picture yourself sitting at the feet of the storyteller. What are your emotions as you listen to this story? What insight does it give you into your own life and concerns?
- Imagine that you are standing in front of the statue of the Mother goddess and that she is speaking to you in your mind. What is she saying to you?
- Visualize yourself as the Mother goddess. Look at the woman standing in front of you with infinite tenderness. How do you want her to feel about herself?

5 **Open your eyes and stretch,** once the experience feels complete. Take some time to write in your journal about what you have experienced and to reflect on its meaning for your life.

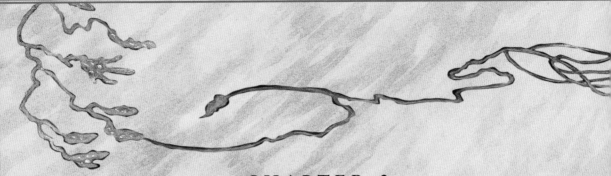

CHAPTER 2

A MERMAID FAIR

* * *

I would be a mermaid fair;

I would sing to myself the whole
of the day;

With a comb of pearl I would
comb my hair;

And still as I comb'd I would sing and say,

'Who is it loves me? Who loves not me?'

I would comb my hair till my ringlets
would fall

Low adown, low adown,

From under my starry sea-bud crown

Low adown and around,

And I should look like a fountain of gold

Springing alone

With a shrill inner sound,

Over the throne

In the midst of the hall;

Till that great sea-snake under the sea

From his coiled sleeps in the central deeps

Would slowly trail himself sevenfold

Round the hall where I sate, and look in
at the gate

With his large calm eyes for the
love of me.

And all the mermen under the sea

Would feel their immortality

Die in their hearts for the love of me.

ALFRED, LORD TENNYSON (1809–1892), 'THE MERMAID'

Tennyson's poem celebrates the mermaid in her most traditional form – as a vain and beautiful woman whose main concern is the way she looks and which men are in love with her. This mermaid's beauty is predatory and causes even immortal mermen to die for her love. When it comes to men, a woman's beauty can be both a blessing and a curse. For a woman, however, authentic beauty comes from within – from living true to who you are.

What is it about a mermaid's beauty that causes men to both desire and fear her? And how can the mermaid help you love your own body, whether or not it conforms to what society considers beautiful?

To answer these questions, this chapter presents mermaid tales from the icy seas of the Orkney Islands north-east of Scotland, where beautiful mermaids wear sealskins rather than fishtails, and from the warm rivers of Nigeria, which are inhabited by handsome mermen as well as lovely mermaids. Both stories illustrate the perils of feminine beauty and reveal what a woman needs in order to feel truly beautiful. Exercises help you explore your feelings about the clothes and jewellery you wear, and give you the chance to gaze into the mermaid's mirror yourself. As you will see, the fair mermaid can teach you to love your authentic beauty exactly as it is.

The Seal Maiden

Among the Celts, Scots and indigenous peoples of north-west America, Siberia and Iceland, mermaids sometimes wear sealskins rather than fishtails. In Britain, sealskin mermaids are called 'selkies'. This traditional story shows how beautiful a woman feels when she is comfortable in her own skin.

* * *

Long ago on the Orkney coast lived Goodman, a strong and handsome young farmer. He was master of a profitable farm, so it is no wonder the beautiful young women of the village batted their eyes and swished their skirts in his direction. But Goodman paid no attention.

When asked why he did not take a wife, Goodman shrugged and said, 'I am no bee to fly heedless to fair flowers. Life is hard enough for a good man without being bewitched by a pretty face and trim ankle.'

One old woman who overheard this oft-repeated explanation remarked, 'Take heed of what you say, young man. For you might find yourself bewitched by the sweet honey of love some fine day.'

One evening Goodman was walking near the shore when he spied a great spotted rock in the sea. Moving closer, he saw a group of women, naked as the day they were born, dancing on the rock's flat top. Heedless of the cold, Goodman waded into the waves until he was close enough to see their honey hair and milk-white skin, shimmering with silver dots like spring salmon.

So beautiful were they, and so graceful their dance, that Goodman was dazzled. As he crept closer still, one by one the women slipped into

sealskins and slid into the sea – all but one, who turned round and round in confusion, seeking the sealskin that Goodman had snatched up and hidden under his cloak.

'Oh, bonnie man,' the Seal Maiden cried, falling to her knees. 'Give me back my sealskin, for I am bone-white and ugly without it and cannot live so.'

'Come home with me and be my wife,' Goodman answered, 'and you shall have pretty clothes aplenty to cover your milk-white skin, and pearl combs for your honey hair.'

Seeing that she had no choice, the Seal Maiden agreed. And for many a year she lived with Goodman and bore him seven children. But though Goodman bought her pretty clothes aplenty and mother-of-pearl combs for her honey hair, many days he came home to find his wife gazing unhappily out to sea.

One evening, as the Seal Maiden sat on the shore in the gathering chill, her youngest daughter came up to her. 'Ma,' she said, 'you're shivery. Why not wrap yourself in the silver fur blanket Da hides in the narrow cupboard?'

With a start, the Seal Maiden jumped up, ran to the cottage, flung open the cupboard and snatched up the sealskin. Kissing her daughter tenderly, she slipped it on and, with a wild cry of joy, plunged into the waves.

When Goodman returned, his oldest daughter told him what had happened. 'So beautiful she looked as she ran, I hadn't the heart to stop her,' she said and, taking her sisters and brothers by the hand, she walked with them down to the shore, where they wept a little as they watched a lithe and lovely silver seal frolic in the foam.

Mermaid Beauty

Men have always been attracted to, and terrified by, beautiful women. The traditional image of the mermaid – a lovely woman perched on a rock, naked but for a wisp of seaweed, gazing at her own face in a looking glass and combing her long, luxurious hair – has been a symbol of that fascination and fear for thousands of years.

* * *

It's easy to see how this image could come to stand for feminine vanity and cruelty. The mermaid with her mirror seems entirely self-focused, her alluring beauty a tease rather than an invitation. Though her breasts are bare, her fishtail closes her off from more intimate contact. Embrace her, and a man risks death by drowning. Marry her (as happens in some tales), and she abandons him to heartbreak if he fails – even accidentally – to honour some agreement between them.

It's worth noting that this view of the mermaid as a vain and cruel beauty was transmitted through paintings, stories and poetry created largely by men. The mermaid in Oscar Wilde's modern fairy tale 'The Fisherman and the Mermaid' (1891) is so beautiful – with hair like a wet fleece of gold, a white ivory body, ears like seashells and lips like sea coral – that the fisherman is willing to send away his soul rather than part from her. Elegantly coiffed and decked out with pearls, a mermaid feeds a male admirer to a fish in a 1906 art poster by French symbolist Gustav Mossa.

The Cult of Beauty as a Curse

However, looked at more deeply – and from a woman's point of view rather than a man's – a mermaid's beauty is often a curse rather than a blessing. It makes strong men seek to possess her, even against her will, as in the 'The Seal Maiden' (see pages 26–27). It leaves her lonely, as in the

Nigerian folktale 'The Fish Husband' (see pages 32–33), in which a very beautiful girl insists that she will marry only a man who is as handsome as she is fair. You will find this story sadly familiar if you know a beautiful woman, who is intelligent, articulate and accomplished, but also forty and lonely – not because she does not want a partner, but because her great beauty attracts men who are seeking a trophy rather than a soulmate, and scares away good men who might truly make her happy.

Worst of all, the cult of beauty turns women against themselves. Psychologists estimate that today 65 per cent of women do not like their bodies. They hate their breasts, they hate their thighs, they hate their hips, they hate their stomachs. Like the Seal Maiden, they feel 'bone-white and ugly' in their own skin. They are obsessed with diets and workouts, with the latest lipstick colours and fashions and hairstyles – though even an expensive facial, a spa pedicure and a new dress may only represent a temporary breakwater against recurring body hatred.

Perhaps the first step to healing a woman's dislike of her body is to remember the original meaning of the mermaid's mirror. Far from being a symbol of self-centred vanity, in the days of the Goddess the symbolic message of looking into a mirror was 'know thyself'. As the Seal Maiden discovered, authentic beauty means knowing who you are at your core – and living true to that knowledge.

Aphrodite's Girdle

How can the mermaid help you to know yourself and love your
authentic beauty exactly as it is?

* * *

For one thing, mermaids remind you of how often women are seen as objects – beautiful things to be admired and possessed – rather than as full human beings. In 'The Seal Maiden' (see pages 26–27) Goodman was not interested in marrying a real girl from his village, no matter how beautiful she was. But he certainly was interested in capturing and possessing a selkie.

Mermaids as objects to be possessed and admired have a grotesque real-life counterpart. Beginning in the late eighteenth century, stuffed mermaids or mermaid-like creatures were often put on display before admiring crowds. In England a young mermaid purportedly caught off the Mexican coast of Acapulco was displayed in a jar at London's Charing Cross,

and a stuffed mermaid brought from Java by a British sea captain was shown at the Turf Coffee House, in London's St James's. At the height of the mermaid craze in 1842, showman Phineas T. Barnum presented a stuffed 'Fejee Mermaid' at New York's Carnegie Hall. So popular was this exhibit that she was later moved to the American Museum in New York.

These mermaid exhibits were obvious hoaxes. But perhaps they are not so far removed from the permed, highlighted, made-up, liposuctioned, depilated and perfumed ideal that many women strive so hard to achieve – an image of beauty created by fashion magazines and television adverts, and no more like a real woman in her natural state than a captured mermaid in a jar.

In the Eye of the Beholder

Who decides, it's important to ask, what makes a woman beautiful? The qualities that a culture considers pleasing vary from place to place and change over time. On islands such as Samoa, large women are considered especially beautiful and dance proudly for visitors, as there is no cultural shame attached to a fat body. As celebrated by Flemish artist Peter Paul Rubens, beautiful women have bulging bellies and full, rounded hips. In Rubens' painting *Hero and Leander* (c. 1607), Hero throws herself into the sea to join her drowned lover Leander, as distinctly plump mermaids lament.

Perhaps women work so hard and spend so much money, time and energy to achieve what society deems to be ideal beauty because, like the mermaid, they are split in half – their minds constantly at war with their bodies. So many women who fail to conform to the current ideal of beauty think of themselves solely in terms of the 'neck up', substituting the satisfaction of intellectual and professional accomplishments for genuine self-love. Alienated from themselves, they feel their bodies to be like a mermaid's lower half: foreign, animal-like, not part of the person they really are.

Healing this split can be lifelong work, but here too the mermaid can help. The mermaid-like Greek goddess Aphrodite had a magic girdle – a sash or belt that, when tied around her waist, had the power to make any man find her beauty irresistible. If you are a woman who dislikes her body, tie a scarf around your hips (like belly dancers do) and imagine that this magic girdle has the power to make you feel irresistibly beautiful – especially to yourself!

The Fish Husband

*The girl in this Yoruba folktale is reminiscent of Goodman (see pages 26–27)
because none of the young men of the village are good enough for her. Here,
too, marriage requires a beautiful sea creature to become a 'fish out of water'.*

* * *

In a village in West Africa lived a very beautiful girl. Because of her loveliness, all the young men in the village courted her, but she would have none of them. 'I will marry only the most handsome man in the land,' she declared. As the years passed, her loneliness grew.

Then one day, while walking along the river, she met a man who was as handsome as she was fair and was immediately enchanted. 'Be my husband,' she said to him boldly, 'because you are the most beautiful man I have ever seen.'

'I would certainly like to marry you,' he replied, 'but I cannot. For I am half-fish and my true home is the river. I only borrow these legs when I wish to walk upon the land. When my visit is done, I must return to the water.'

'No matter,' said the girl. 'You can borrow those strong legs and visit me secretly from time to time, so long as each time you come, you look as handsome as you do this minute.'

And so they were married, and from time to time the fish husband visited his beautiful wife. The pair sat together on the bank of the river eating sweets. The fish husband told the girl about his palace of silver and gems under the flowing waters, and brought her gifts from the sea: pearl necklaces and coral earrings and cowrie shells for her hair. The girl sang for

her husband the songs of her people and told him stories. No one in the village could explain why, but everyone could see that the girl was happy again.

Then one day the girl's father came to her and told her that he had arranged for her to marry a young man from a neighbouring village. 'He is handsome and strong,' the father assured her, 'and it's high time you became a wife.'

Seeing that she had no choice, the girl told her father about her fish husband and begged him to bless their marriage, because she loved him so and could not live without him.

Her father pretended to agree, but later he told the girl's brother to follow her and do what needed to be done to protect his sister from her monstrous husband. The next day, when the girl was happily embracing her fish husband, her brother jumped out from behind a bush and stabbed him. As the girl watched in horror, her husband's strong legs

shrivelled into a scaly fishtail and he sank into the river and disappeared.

Instantly the surface of the river turned blood-red. In terrible grief, the girl cried out, 'I will join the spirit of my beloved husband' and jumped into the rushing waters. But she did not drown. Instead, her lovely legs fused together and grew silver-green scales, and she became a mermaid – an *onijegi* in the Yoruba tongue. People who live along the river say that, even today, she can be heard singing to her fish husband.

Clothes as Sealskins

Exploring your attitudes and feelings about the clothes and jewellery you choose helps you to understand the external ways you express your authentic inner beauty. These insights can make you feel more at ease in whatever you wear. Like a selkie's sealskin, a woman's clothes have the power to make her feel beautiful. Think about the answers to the following questions, or note your answers in your journal. Keep any insights in mind the next time you shop for clothes.

* * *

HERE'S WHAT TO DO

1 **Travel in your mind** back to your childhood. What was your favourite piece of clothing? How did you feel when you were wearing it? What does it say about the grown-up person you have become?

2 **Still travelling** through your memories, what outfit or piece of clothing that you have worn has made you feel the most beautiful? Allow your mind to revisit the occasion when you wore it. What current feelings does this memory evoke?

3 **Consider your current wardrobe.** What are your favourite pieces of clothing? What qualities make them special? If there is something in your wardrobe in which you feel particularly unattractive, don't wait: give it away!

4 **What thoughts and feelings** do you have while getting dressed? Are you aware of dressing to please someone other than yourself? How would your style change if you dressed solely to please yourself?

5 **Picture yourself** wearing an imaginary outfit that makes you feel irresistibly beautiful. Scan your body from head to toe, paying careful attention to each part: hair and make-up, jewellery, combs or hair ribbons, scarves or belts, underclothes and outer clothes, stockings and shoes. What does this outfit reveal about your values and your dreams – about the woman you are at your core?

Gifts from the Sea

Wearing jewellery that is a gift from the sea can make you feel especially beautiful, perhaps because it links you to the natural feminine powers of the deep. Pearls, coral and cowrie shells, such as the fish husband brought as gifts to his human wife, are particularly potent choices.

* * *

HERE'S WHAT TO DO

Consider the following natural gifts and the benefits they can offer you:

• **Pearls** symbolize purity, serenity, integrity and wisdom. From a rough grain of sand, a pearl is transformed slowly over time into an object of great value and beauty. Wearing pearls stimulates your femininity, lifts your spirits and helps you to feel more calm and centred. Try wearing a single pearl teardrop necklace, a pearl ring or pearl earrings the next time you want to feel especially feminine and serene.

• **Coral** symbolizes life and blood energy. Ancient peoples believed in the invigorating and protective powers of coral and used it to make amulets for children. You may find that wearing coral jewellery soothes your fears and tensions, helps to overcome depression and stimulates your vital energies. When you are feeling low, wear a coral necklace or bracelet against your bare skin and let its warmth kindle the natural beauty of your spirit.

• **Cowrie shells,** with their deep cleft and inward curve, are especially feminine. In ancient cultures, cowries symbolized fertility and were given to brides to guarantee healthy children. In China and Africa cowrie shells were used as money. In Nigeria the cowrie is also a mouth that speaks the lessons of the Orisas, or gods; Yoruba folktales such as 'The Fish Husband' (see pages 32–33) are traditionally called 'cowrie tales'. Wear a cowrie necklace when you seek greater abundance and fertile creativity.

The Mermaid's Mirror

For this exercise you will need a round hand mirror, a hairbrush or large comb and a full-length mirror. Do this exercise at a time when you can have complete privacy, perhaps in the evening after a relaxing bath or shower. Your clothes should be loose, comfortable and easy to take off; a soft robe would be a perfect choice. Make sure the room is comfortably warm.

* * *

HERE'S WHAT TO DO

1 **Sit comfortably,** holding up your hand mirror and looking into your eyes. Pay attention to any feelings that arise as you examine your face and its features.
- What do your eyes reveal about your feelings?
- What does your facial expression say about your mood?
- What thoughts, feelings, attitudes or beliefs arise when you look at your eyes, nose, lips and hair? Pay special attention to any painful or negative feelings.

2 **Pick up the hairbrush or comb** and brush or comb your hair slowly and gently. What feelings, thoughts or memories arise as you do so?

3 **Remove your robe** and stand in front of the full-length mirror. It's fine to close your eyes at first, if doing so makes this step easier. Slowly open your eyes and look at your reflection. Don't be surprised if strong feelings arise, especially if you are not used to seeing yourself naked. Pay attention to what you are experiencing, without pushing any feelings, whether positive or negative, away.

4 **Scan your body,** starting at the top.
- Look at your head. What is your state of mind? What thoughts are arising?
- Look at your shoulders. Are they relaxed or tight? What tensions are they holding?
- Look at your right arm and right hand. What do they want to say to you?
- Look at your left arm and left hand. Is their message different from that of the right? How?
- Look at your chest. Is it sunken or proud?
- Look at your navel and belly. What feelings and attitudes reside there?

- Look at your hips. So many stories live here: what are yours?
- Look at your knees. Are they locked or loose? What strains are they carrying?
- Look at your feet. How do they move you? Do they shuffle or strut? Jog or dance?

5 **Take a step back** after your scan and look at your body as a whole. Try to see what is really there, rather than what you think *should* be there. Pay special attention to any attitudes or beliefs you may be holding about your body: my breasts are too small; my thighs are too fat; I hate my freckles.

6 **Remind yourself** as you look at your body of the many things it has done – and can do – and of how well it has served you. Can you look yourself in the eyes and say honestly, 'I like my body' and 'My body is beautiful'? If not, set the intention that you will be able to do so some day.

7 **Put on your robe** and take some time to write in your journal about what you have discovered.

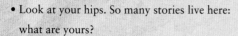

CHAPTER 3
THE MERMAID'S SONG

* * *

Full fathom five thy father lies;

Of his bones are coral made;

Those are pearls that were his eyes;

Nothing of him that doth fade

But doth suffer a sea-change

Into something rich and strange.

Sea-nymphs hourly ring his knell

Ding-dong.

Hark! now I hear them – Ding-dong, bell.

WILLIAM SHAKESPEARE (1564–1616),
THE TEMPEST

The sea has the power to transform, Shakespeare writes in this song from *The Tempest*. It can change even death into a thing of beauty. Personal creativity has a similar power: art can help you transform any experience, sensation or feeling into 'something rich and strange'. Using your creativity also changes you. Spending time on your own forms of creative expression can work a 'sea-change' on your life and help you transform every day into a work of art.

How has the mermaid's song inspired great art? And how can the mermaid muse inspire you to delve into your own creativity?

In this chapter you will read two very different tales about the mermaid's song: the story of the Rhinemaidens, the singing mermaids who guard a golden treasure in Richard Wagner's *Ring* opera cycle, and a charming folktale about a Swiss mermaid who falls in love with a cowherd and learns to yodel. The message of these stories is that personal creativity arises from deep within, and that expressing yourself creatively is both joyful and liberating. You will also explore how adopting the mermaid as your muse can help you vanquish the sea monsters that may be blocking your creativity. With these blocks removed, your inner mermaid can find her voice and express her wisdom.

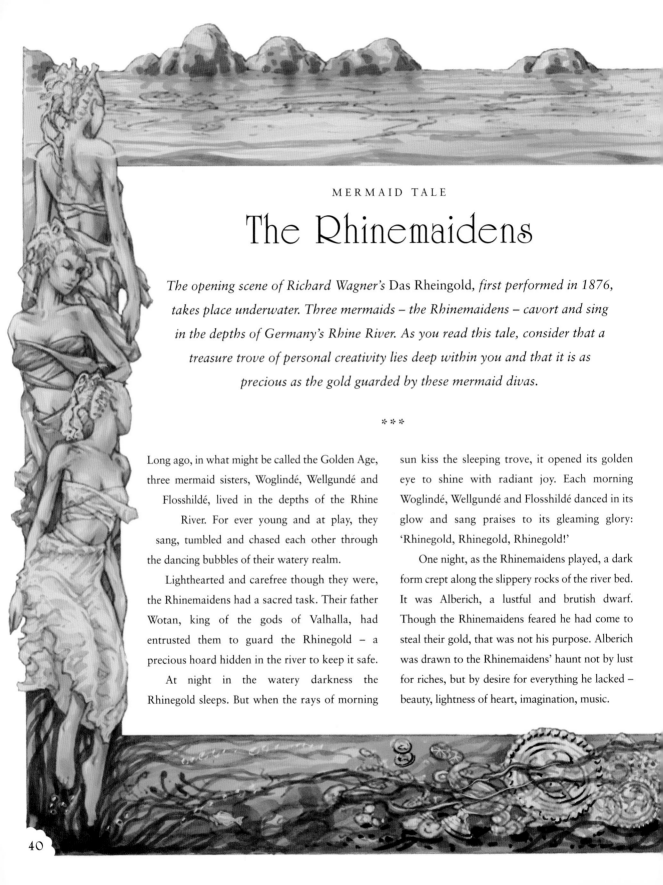

The Rhinemaidens

The opening scene of Richard Wagner's Das Rheingold, *first performed in 1876, takes place underwater. Three mermaids – the Rhinemaidens – cavort and sing in the depths of Germany's Rhine River. As you read this tale, consider that a treasure trove of personal creativity lies deep within you and that it is as precious as the gold guarded by these mermaid divas.*

* * *

Long ago, in what might be called the Golden Age, three mermaid sisters, Woglindé, Wellgundé and Flosshildé, lived in the depths of the Rhine River. For ever young and at play, they sang, tumbled and chased each other through the dancing bubbles of their watery realm.

Lighthearted and carefree though they were, the Rhinemaidens had a sacred task. Their father Wotan, king of the gods of Valhalla, had entrusted them to guard the Rhinegold – a precious hoard hidden in the river to keep it safe.

At night in the watery darkness the Rhinegold sleeps. But when the rays of morning sun kiss the sleeping trove, it opened its golden eye to shine with radiant joy. Each morning Woglindé, Wellgundé and Flosshildé danced in its glow and sang praises to its gleaming glory: 'Rhinegold, Rhinegold, Rhinegold!'

One night, as the Rhinemaidens played, a dark form crept along the slippery rocks of the river bed. It was Alberich, a lustful and brutish dwarf. Though the Rhinemaidens feared he had come to steal their gold, that was not his purpose. Alberich was drawn to the Rhinemaidens' haunt not by lust for riches, but by desire for everything he lacked – beauty, lightness of heart, imagination, music.

When Alberich offered himself as their sweetheart, the Rhinemaidens giggled with relief. A lover was no threat, for, as they foolishly explained to Alberich, the Rhinegold can be forged into a ring of power only by a person willing to forswear love completely. Adept at love play, each Rhinemaiden in turn pretended to fall in love with Alberich, luring him on with honeyed promises.

'You are as wise as you are handsome,' Woglindé teased.

'Come closer so that I can embrace you,' Wellgundé urged.

'Masterful man, make me your own,' Flosshildé sang seductively.

But just as the dwarf was about to seize his amorous playmate, each slithered from his grasp and swam away, taunting him for his ugliness and awkwardness.

'Cruel and heartless creatures,' Alberich muttered darkly. 'I can only take so much! If you won't love me, I'll try the pleasure of power.' And with that, he ripped the Rhinegold from its rocky hiding place and swore a mighty oath cursing love for ever!

'Rhinegold, Rhinegold, Rhinegold!' Woglindé, Wellgundé and Flosshildé sang in despair, 'our light, our life, our joy. Gone from us. Woe!'

Forged into a magical ring and lusted after by gods and human heroes, the ring became the centrepiece of a vast epic of greed and power, love and redemption. In the final scene, Brünnhilde, the Valkyrie heroine, takes the ring from her dead hero-lover Siegfried's finger as he lies on a funeral pyre. As the flames consume Valhalla, ushering in the twilight of the gods, the Rhine rises to wash the world clean, and the Rhinemaidens reclaim their golden treasure.

The Mermaid as Muse

Mermaids and their lore have inspired creative artists, writers and composers from ancient times to the present day. In early productions of Wagner's Das Rheingold, *the Rhinemaidens were supported on wheeled carts that gave them the illusion of floating in scenery waves. A contemporary production has them suspended from bungee cords, on which they twirl and spin in exuberant underwater play.*

* * *

Once you start to look for them, you will see mermaid images everywhere: on Classical vases, bronzes and terracotta reliefs; on Roman mosaics, frescos and wood carvings; on medieval coats of arms, decorative tiles and illustrated manuscripts; on fine-art oils and watercolours; on jewellery and glassware; on ship's figureheads and weathervanes; in contemporary book illustrations and film posters. It's a safe bet that you have probably seen a mermaid image recently, on the green and white logo of the international coffee-shop chain where you bought your *latte*!

In the Middle Ages the mermaid, as an allegory of the deadly consequences of lust, inspired the woodcarvers and stonemasons who decorated churches and cathedrals. During the Renaissance, rediscovery of the Classical gods and goddesses brought the mermaid into the paintings of Raphael and other masters. In the nineteenth century Pre-Raphaelite painters such as John Waterhouse, Edward Burne-Jones and John Collier saw the haunting and mystical beauty of the mermaid as a perfect symbol of the intertwining of love and death. In the twentieth century surrealist painters such as René Magritte playfully painted her lounging on an upholstered divan and, famously, on the seashore as a fish above the waist and a human woman below.

This wealth of mermaid art is not surprising, given that in Greek mythology the goddesses charged with inspiring creativity through the arts are the Muses – the nine daughters of Zeus, king of the gods, and Mnemosyne, goddess of memory. Said to inhabit sacred springs at Mount Helicon and Delphi, among other places, the Muses are water nymphs – close cousins to the mermaid. No wonder artists of all kinds the world over have found mermaids to be a constant source of creative inspiration.

Follow your own Muse

You can also adopt the mermaid as your muse. The waters of creative self-expression brim with potential ideas and projects, fed by your experiences and memories, your emotions and dreams. There are as many ways of expressing your creativity as there are fish in the ocean. The colours and fabrics you use to decorate your home, the recipes you devise and the meals you prepare, your choice of clothing and accessories, the choreography of your daily exercise routine – all these are as much a celebration of personal creativity as any poem or story, sketch or painting.

The mermaid muse also reminds you that the true source of creative expression lies deep within you. She invites you to plunge into your feelings and to find original ways to bring the treasures of your personal style and view of the world to the surface. Her joyful underwater acrobatics carry the message that creativity liberates your spirit and gives you the opportunity to swim freely as you please, beyond the constraints of everyday routine and responsibilities.

Mermaids and your Creativity

How can mermaids inspire and support your creativity? First, it's important to recognize that in order to create art, you need to immerse yourself in the images that surround you. Images – everything you see, hear, taste, smell and touch, the remembered or imaginary re-creation of these experiences and the feelings that they invoke – are the essential raw materials of art.

* * *

Paradoxically, the imagery from which creativity springs is both within you and all around you. Inner images rise into conscious awareness through dreams, memories, fantasies and imaginative associations. Keeping a dream journal or capturing – through sketches, doodles or notes – the images and associations that arise spontaneously from within helps to keep your creative imagination flowing.

Images from the world outside become available for art whenever you pay real attention to the experiences of daily life: to the shades of green on the trees rushing past the window of your commuter train, the textures of the fabrics in a dress shop, the earthy smell of the potato you are peeling and the tart sweetness of the strawberry on your cereal. Visualizing yourself as a mermaid swimming mindfully in a sea of inner and outer imagery stocks the pool of your imagination with a rich abundance of creative fish.

Take the Plunge

The only way to get into the creative flow is to jump in and start swimming. Thinking about writing a story or planning to paint watercolours

just won't do. If your dream is to write, get out your notebook or fire up your computer and start writing. If nothing comes, write about the idea that you have nothing to say, and the feelings that arise from that thought. If you long to draw, take your sketchbook to the beach and draw whatever swims past. Imagine, if you like, that you are a mermaid visiting the human world for the first time. Describe or draw your experiences as if everything were unusual and delightful. The mermaid in 'Hansi and the Nix' (see pages 46–47) finds the yodelling of a Swiss cowherd so enchanting that she re-creates an entire town to keep him from getting homesick.

Finally, keep a sharp eye out for sea monsters. These enemies to personal creativity are both cunning and treacherous. They whisper that you are blocked and always will be; they hiss that you have no talent; they scold that you have more important things to do than waste your time on all this creative nonsense; they warn that your partner or children will think you're crazy if you enrol in a photography class, enter a poetry contest or audition for a part with the local theatre group.

One good way to overcome creative blocks is to invite them to tea. Rather than trying to argue down your negative voices or steamroller over them, try giving them a chance to tell you their story. Put on your favourite music and dance the feeling of being blocked and the feeling of swimming in the creative flow. Take photographs that symbolize breaking through your blocks: a bubbling fountain or a flower growing from a crack in the concrete. In other words, grab hold of the tail of your sea monster and let it pull you deeper into the creative sea.

Hansi and the Nix

This charming folktale is unusual in that it tells of a mermaid who is enchanted by a mortal's song. The mermaid is a nix, a water nymph that lives in European springs and rivers. Her child-like delight at the sights and sounds of the Swiss countryside recalls the attention to sensory experience that primes the pump of creativity.

* * *

In the lake of Zug in central Switzerland there once lived a nix. During the warm afternoons of summer she liked to sit by the shore of the lake, combing her hair and admiring the reflection of the mountains in the clear water. One fine day, when daisies dotted the hillsides and the snowcaps gleamed white against the azure sky, the nix sat beside the lake singing a song she had heard cowherds using to call their brown cows to the barn for evening milking.

When she reached the last line of the song, a strong male voice joined in from behind her. And when she ran out of melody, the voice continued, 'Hol-de-ree-dee-ah.'

'What's a Hol-de-ree-dee-ah?' the nix asked, turning around to face the young man and his brown cow standing behind her.

'It's a yodel,' the young man said, grinning. 'A yodel is how that song is supposed to end. I should know, because I'm a cowherd. My name is Hansi, and that's the song I use to call my cow Klara at milking time.'

'You can call me Nixie,' the nix said, smiling, for Hansi was very handsome. 'And I should like to know how to yodel, because nixies love to sing. Teach me, please.'

So Hansi did. Each afternoon of summer, Hansi and the nix sat by the shores of Lake Zug

practising yodelling, while Klara munched dandelions nearby. But when autumn came, the nix shivered in the cool alpine air. 'Come with me to the bottom of the lake,' she said. 'It's warm and cosy there.'

At first Hansi hesitated. He had heard that young men who follow mermaids never return. But he was fond of Nixie and so he agreed. Soon he was happily yodelling with Nixie under the lake, rather than beside it. But when the winter winds began to blow, Hansi became unhappy. 'I'm worried about Klara,' he told Nixie. 'She could be cold in her icy barn.'

'Is that all?' Nixie replied. 'I'll fetch your cow for you.' And so she did and also brought Hansi anything he asked for: wheels of ripe Swiss cheese, his rocking chair and feather bed, his alpenhorn and fishing pole – whatever he pined for. But the more things the nix brought Hansi, the more he wanted, and soon Nixie was so busy bringing things to Hansi that there was no time for yodelling.

Then one day the nix was gone a long time. When Hansi awoke, he could not believe his eyes. To make sure he had everything he would ever want, Nixie had enchanted the entire town of Zug and brought it down to the bottom of the lake! Even today, on summer afternoons, you can see the streets and houses of Zug beneath the water. And, if you listen carefully, you can hear a mermaid yodelling 'Hol-de-ree-dee-ah.'

Sea Monsters

Perhaps you long to dive into your own creativity and bring its treasures to the surface. But your urge to write, paint, dance or sing is blocked by sea monsters of fear and self-doubt. To overcome creative blocks, first you need to become aware of the personal monsters that keep you from your creativity and explore their origins.

* * *

HERE'S WHAT TO DO

1 **Jot down a list** of the negative beliefs that inhibit your creative impulses. For instance, 'I can't draw / can't write'; 'My ideas aren't good enough'; 'I'm too old to learn singing / playwriting / tango dancing.'

2 **Circle the three most potent beliefs,** the ones that cause a heavy feeling in your chest when you read through the list.

3 **Choose one of these monsters** and write the story of how it came into your life. Perhaps your monster is the second-year teacher who held up your artwork and explained to the class why the cow you had painted was 'all wrong'. Write about the room you were in, what you were wearing, what was said and how you felt about it.

4 **Draw a picture of your monster,** or cut out a picture from a magazine that captures the feeling of that incident.

5 **Perform some action** that symbolizes your intention to vanquish this monster. Crumple up your picture and burn it. Draw a circle around it, cross it out with a big red X and hang it on the wall. Or write a letter to the child artist you were, giving yourself permission to draw a cow any way you like.

The Sensory Sea

The sea of creativity is alive with sensory wonders. The vivid neon of tropical fish, the sinuous sway of sea plants and the rhythmic splash of waves on rocks can stimulate your senses and inspire creative exploration. There are numerous ways to dive in.

* * *

HERE'S WHAT TO DO

- **Visit a farmers' market** or greengrocer's. Breathe in the smell of peaches and potatoes; thump the melons and run your fingers over the rind of avocados; count the colours of the apples. Bring home a few samples, including some fruits or vegetables you have never tasted. Enjoy each one with your full attention. Write a poem describing the experience, sketch your favourite or create a new recipe starring your discovery.

- **Take a walk in nature,** looking for the special signs of the season. In winter, examine the ice crystals on a tree branch and listen to the crunch of your feet on the frozen ground. In spring, gently uncurl the fern fronds and inhale the moist warmth of fresh dirt. Bring home something that inspires you: a rock speckled with moss, a crimson leaf, an abandoned snail shell. Hold the object in your hand and listen for its story. Write or sketch or dance or sing what you hear.

- **Treat yourself to a culture feast.** Spend the afternoon in an art gallery, eat a meal in an unfamiliar ethnic restaurant, or attend a concert, opera, ballet or theatre performance. The next day write the story of a character in a painting. Sketch in a cubist or impressionist style. Listen to a new kind of music. Cook an ethnic meal for friends. Sign up for dance lessons.

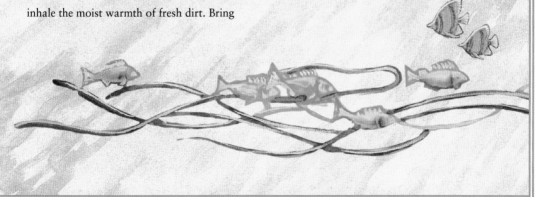

Converse with a Mermaid Image

Conversing with an artistic image is a wonderful way to access the inner voice that can help you discover who you are. The voice that answers when you enter into dialogue with an artistic image is, of course, your own voice, not some supernatural entity. You might think of it as the voice of your soul, your deep intuition or, in this context, your wise inner mermaid.

For this exercise you could use the mermaid you created in response to 'Picture your Mermaid Self' (see page 21); a new mermaid that you paint or draw for this exercise; or any of the mermaid illustrations in this book to which you feel especially drawn. You could also use any other mermaid painting you like. You will need your journal or a notebook.

* * *

HERE'S WHAT TO DO

1 **Place the mermaid image** you have chosen in front of you. Then sit comfortably, close your eyes and take several deep breaths, focusing your attention on the rise and fall of your abdomen as you breathe in and out.

2 **Slowly open your eyes** and look at the mermaid image you have chosen, once you are feeling relaxed and centred in your body. Take enough time to study the image carefully, paying attention to the details of the setting, the colours and the forms. Take note in particular of the mermaid's posture, gestures and facial expression. Look into her eyes.

3 **Now close your eyes again** and imagine that the image is coming alive or taking on a life of its own.

4 **Focus on one aspect** of the mermaid image as you open your eyes, such as her face, gestures or expression, or on a particular detail, such as the colour of the water or the shape of the rocks or waves.

5 **Ask this aspect of the image** what it would like to tell you. Be patient, keep your mind open and wait for the answer. When words start to flow, take your notebook and write down whatever comes in a steady stream, without stopping to read what you have written or to edit the response.

6 **Take the time to go deeper** by asking additional questions and writing down the responses, if the message you receive feels as if it has a connection to other past or present circumstances in your life. For instance:

• When in my life have I experienced a similar feeling?

• What past or present habits or behaviours may be related?

• What advice am I being given?

7 **When you have explored fully** one aspect of the image, move on to another part. Continue this process until you have conversed with every part of the image or until the process seems complete.

8 **To conclude,** ask the image as a whole to tell you something that may relate to who you are – or who you are meant to be. Give up any preconceptions about what you would like to hear, and write down the response without judging or censoring it.

9 **Reflect on the answers** you have received, taking as much time as you need to do so.

CHAPTER 4
MERMAID LOVE

* * *

'Twas on the deep Atlantic,

Midst equinoctial gales;

This young farmer fell overboard

Among the sharks and whales;

He disappeared so quickly,

So headlong down went he,

That he went out of sight

Like a streak of light

To the bottom of the deep blue sea.

We lowered a boat to find him,

We thought to see his corpse,

When up to the top he came
with a bang,

And sang in a voice so hoarse,

'My comrades and my messmates,

Oh, do not weep for me,

For I'm married to a mermaid,

At the bottom of the deep blue sea.'

ARTHUR LLOYD (1839–1904), 'MARRIED TO A MERMAID'

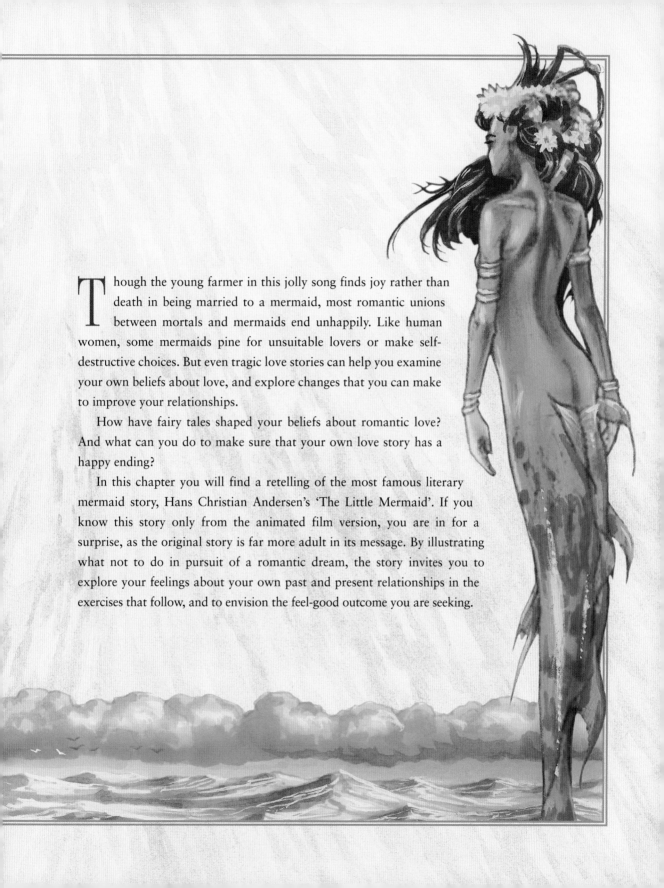

Though the young farmer in this jolly song finds joy rather than death in being married to a mermaid, most romantic unions between mortals and mermaids end unhappily. Like human women, some mermaids pine for unsuitable lovers or make self-destructive choices. But even tragic love stories can help you examine your own beliefs about love, and explore changes that you can make to improve your relationships.

How have fairy tales shaped your beliefs about romantic love? And what can you do to make sure that your own love story has a happy ending?

In this chapter you will find a retelling of the most famous literary mermaid story, Hans Christian Andersen's 'The Little Mermaid'. If you know this story only from the animated film version, you are in for a surprise, as the original story is far more adult in its message. By illustrating what not to do in pursuit of a romantic dream, the story invites you to explore your feelings about your own past and present relationships in the exercises that follow, and to envision the feel-good outcome you are seeking.

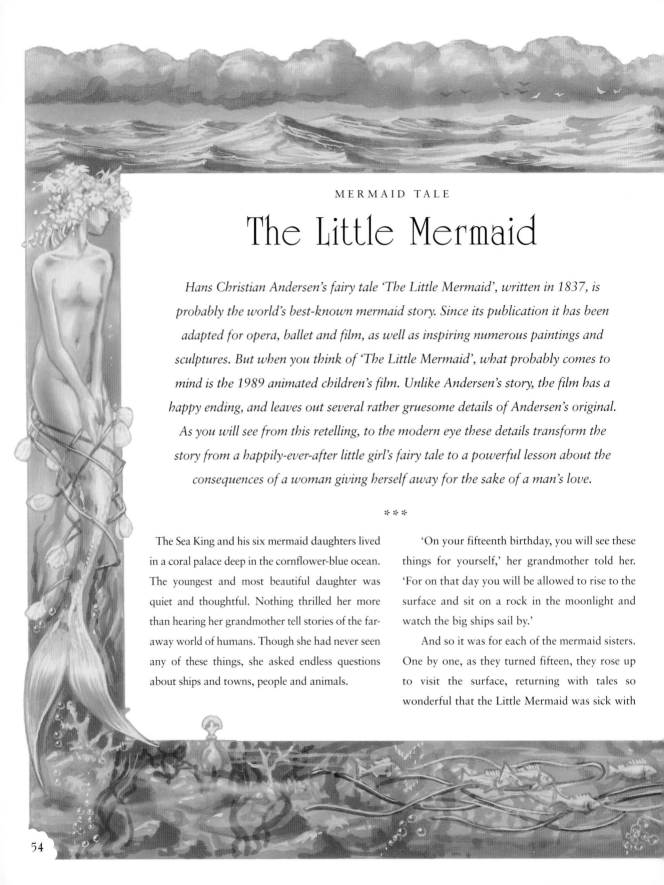

The Little Mermaid

Hans Christian Andersen's fairy tale 'The Little Mermaid', written in 1837, is probably the world's best-known mermaid story. Since its publication it has been adapted for opera, ballet and film, as well as inspiring numerous paintings and sculptures. But when you think of 'The Little Mermaid', what probably comes to mind is the 1989 animated children's film. Unlike Andersen's story, the film has a happy ending, and leaves out several rather gruesome details of Andersen's original. As you will see from this retelling, to the modern eye these details transform the story from a happily-ever-after little girl's fairy tale to a powerful lesson about the consequences of a woman giving herself away for the sake of a man's love.

✳ ✳ ✳

The Sea King and his six mermaid daughters lived in a coral palace deep in the cornflower-blue ocean. The youngest and most beautiful daughter was quiet and thoughtful. Nothing thrilled her more than hearing her grandmother tell stories of the far-away world of humans. Though she had never seen any of these things, she asked endless questions about ships and towns, people and animals.

'On your fifteenth birthday, you will see these things for yourself,' her grandmother told her. 'For on that day you will be allowed to rise to the surface and sit on a rock in the moonlight and watch the big ships sail by.'

And so it was for each of the mermaid sisters. One by one, as they turned fifteen, they rose up to visit the surface, returning with tales so wonderful that the Little Mermaid was sick with

longing. She stood in the open window of the palace, looking up through the dark water and stretching out her white hands towards shadows that she imagined were ships full of people sailing overhead. She wanted to cry, but mermaids have no tears, and so they suffer all the more.

At last it was her turn. Her grandmother put a heavy wreath of pearl-bedecked white lilies in her hair and decorated her fishtail with eight big oysters to show that she was a princess.

'But they hurt,' the Little Mermaid cried.

'One must suffer to be beautiful,' her grandmother replied.

The Little Mermaid made no further protest. 'Goodbye,' she said and rose quickly to the surface until, for the first time, she saw the clouds gleam red and gold at sunset and the evening star shine in the sky. Near her, a large ship lay at anchor. Peering through a cabin window, she saw many richly dressed people, but the handsomest of all was a young prince, whose sixteenth birthday was being celebrated with music and fireworks. The Little Mermaid could not tear her eyes away from his noble forehead and dark eyes.

The Little Mermaid Saves the Prince

Suddenly the sky darkened, lightning flashed and a terrible storm blew up. The ship plunged wildly until a wave, high as a black mountain, snapped the main mast, and the ship heeled over and broke apart. Heedless of floating beams and planks of wood, the Little Mermaid searched the raging water until she found the Prince. His strength was failing and he surely would have died, but she held his head above the water and let the waves carry them to shore.

The Prince's eyes were closed as the Little Mermaid laid him on the sand, kissing him again and again. When bells began to ring in a big white building nearby, she hid behind a rock and watched as a beautiful young girl knelt by the Prince and cradled his head until he opened his eyes and smiled at her. Then the Little Mermaid was very sad, for the Prince did not know that it was she who had saved him.

Returning to her father's palace, the Little Mermaid felt her love for the Prince grow till she could think of little else. She had always been quiet and thoughtful, but now she

55

spent most days alone. She surfaced many times near the sandy beach where she had left the Prince, but he was never there, and she returned home more dejected than before.

Then, when her lovesick sadness was more than she could bear, she confided in one of her sisters, who, of course, told the others. Then one morning, as the Little Mermaid sat in her garden hugging the marble statue of a young man she had found in a shipwreck that reminded her of the Prince, her sisters came to find her.

'Come little sister,' they said. 'We have a surprise.' Linking arms, the mermaid sisters rose to the surface near a grand palace, with a magnificent marble staircase that led right down to the sea. Most marvellous of all, the Prince himself was standing on a balcony gazing out to sea.

Now that the Little Mermaid knew where he lived, many evenings she returned to the Prince's palace to hide in the green rushes and watch the Prince sail his graceful boat with music on board and flags waving. The more she saw of human beings, the more she longed to live among them.

Many nights the Little Mermaid watched near the palace where the Prince lived, to catch a glimpse of him. She asked her grandmother endless questions.

'Do human beings live for ever?' she asked one day.

'No,' her grandmother answered. 'Their lives are much shorter than ours. We live for three hundred years and then turn into foam upon the water. Human beings live for less than a hundred, but their immortal souls rise up to the stars after the body dies.'

'I wish I had a human soul,' the Little Mermaid said sadly.

'Better not think of it,' her grandmother replied. 'That could happen only if a man loved you with all his heart and married you for all eternity. On that day, part of his soul would flow into your body. But that will never happen. A man would find your fishtail ugly. Up there you must have legs to be beautiful.'

The Little Mermaid looked dejectedly at her fishtail. 'I will visit the Sea Witch,' she whispered to herself. 'Perhaps she can help me.'

The Little Mermaid Consults the Sea Witch

To reach the house of the Sea Witch, the Little Mermaid had to swim through a fearful forest of polyps, whose writhing arms like hundred-headed snakes and whose fingers like wriggling worms tried to grab her. Already in their slimy grasp were the bleached bones of drowned men and, most terrifying of all, a little mermaid they had caught and strangled.

'I know why you have come,' said the Sea Witch, on whose horrible bosom fat water snakes were crawling, showing their yellow bellies. 'Stupidly you want to get rid of your fishtail and have two stumps for walking, so that the Prince may fall in love with you and give you part of his soul.' She laughed loudly and hideously. 'I will make you a potion that will split your fishtail and shrink it into legs. But I warn you: every step you take will be as painful as

stepping on a sharp knife! Are you willing to suffer this?'

The Little Mermaid nodded.

'And remember,' said the Witch, 'if you fail to win the Prince's love, then on the first morning after he has married another, your heart will break and you will turn into foam upon the water.'

'I will do it,' said the Little Mermaid, her face as pale as death.

'But, my pretty little Princess, you must pay me with the best thing you possess. You have the most beautiful voice of anyone who lives under the sea. I must have it for my precious potion.'

The Little Mermaid trembled. 'But if you take away my voice, what have I got left?'

'Your lovely figure, your graceful movement and your eloquent eyes,' said the Sea Witch.

Thinking only of the Prince, the Little Mermaid put out her little tongue for the witch to cut off, and took the vial of potion.

On the marble steps of the Prince's palace, the Little Mermaid drank the potion. It went through her tender body like a two-edged sword, and she fainted from the pain. When she awoke, the Prince was kneeling over her. She wrapped her long hair around her naked body, now with its two beautiful white legs, took his hand and walked with him into the palace. Every step was like walking on sharp knives, but she bore the pain gladly.

Though she could not speak, the Prince was enchanted with the Little Mermaid. Ladies dressed her in silks, and she danced for the Prince again and again. Each time she rose onto her toes, she felt as if she were treading on pointed needles. The Prince had a page's uniform made for her and let her sleep on a velvet cushion just outside his door. He took her along with him to ride on horseback through the woods. When the Little Mermaid heard the birds singing among the leaves, she thought, 'Oh, how I wish I could sing for him. If only the Prince knew that I have given away my beautiful voice forever to be with him!' With the Prince, she climbed high mountains. Though her tender feet bled so that all could see, still she smiled. 'I will care for him, love him and give up my life for him,' she said to herself.

The Prince Marries

The Prince loved the Little Mermaid as he might love a good, sweet child, but it never occurred to him to marry her. He had given his heart to the young maiden who had found him on the beach and who, the Prince thought, had saved his life. When it was time for him to marry, his parents arranged for him to meet the daughter of a neighbouring king, who had just returned from being schooled at a holy convent.

When the Prince saw his intended bride he was overjoyed. 'You are she,' he said and clasped her in his arms. Church bells pealed, and the

Trembling, the Little Mermaid drew back the purple curtain and gazed at the Prince, who was asleep with his lovely bride's head on his breast. She bent down and kissed him on the forehead. The knife shook in her hands, but then the Prince murmured his bride's name in a dream and, in despair, the Little Mermaid flung the knife into the sea and then threw herself over the rail.

The Little Mermaid is Saved

She felt her body dissolve to foam, but then she was lifted up by hundreds of beautiful transparent beings.

'Where am I going?' she asked.

'To the daughters of the air,' they answered. 'We do good deeds, bringing comfort to suffering humans. After three hundred years of doing all the good we can, we win an immortal soul. You have struggled bravely and can join us in the spiritual world.'

Hearing these words, for the first time the Little Mermaid began to cry.

Little Mermaid, dressed in silk and gold held the bride's train as the happy couple exchanged vows. She accompanied them to the ship, where a tent of purple and gold had been placed for the bridal pair to rest on their wedding night.

Late that night, as the Little Mermaid stood at the rail knowing that it was her last night of life, she saw her sisters rise out of the waves, their beautiful hair cut off. 'We gave our hair to the Sea Witch in return for this magic knife,' they said. 'Plunge it into the Prince's heart. When his warm blood sprinkles your feet, you will be a mermaid again and can come home.'

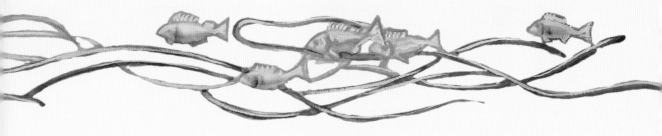

The True Nature of Love

*'I know the perfect man for me is out there. Is it you?' reads the plaintive
personal ad placed by a 45-year-old woman who signs herself 'Sleeping Beauty'.
It seems that, no matter how grown-up they are, or how disillusioning their life
circumstances have been, women of every age cling to the ideal of happily-ever-after
romantic love. Fairy tales like 'The Little Mermaid' (see pages 54–59) have
helped to create and perpetuate this fantasy.*

* * *

Unlike most of the other mermaid tales in this book, the story of 'The Little Mermaid' is a negative example – a heartbreaking parable of how misunderstanding the true nature of love can cause a woman to give up her power and sacrifice her wholeness for the sake of a man. However, by looking closely at the story's background and implications, and by using it as an invitation to explore your own beliefs about love, 'The Little Mermaid' can help you stay on a firmer footing with your own romantic partners.

Although it is a literary story rather than a folktale, in writing it Andersen drew on traditional mermaid lore, skilfully combined with his observations about human nature and elements of his own psychology and life story. From traditional lore, dating back at least to the writings of the Swiss alchemist, physician and scholar Paracelsus (1493–1541), Andersen drew the idea that mermaids were equal to human beings in all respects, except that they lacked a soul. The means for gaining a soul, according to this tradition, was through marriage to a mortal man.

It's tempting to laugh at this notion and breathe a sigh of relief at how far women have come. But the idea that a man is a complete being – and that a

woman becomes complete only when she unites with him – is long-standing and still devastating for many women. You probably know accomplished and successful women who believe at some level that their 'real' life will begin when they finally meet and marry the man of their dreams.

Loss of Soul

Like the Little Mermaid, these women lack a soul, in the sense that they have given over responsibility for their wholeness to someone else. The Prince's soul can flow into the Little Mermaid because she herself is empty. She believes that marriage will grant her access to a life that is infinitely larger and more wonderful than her own. It's not hard to see that a woman who gives up her professional ambitions to put her husband through medical school, or who leaves a job or a home she loves to follow him on a numbing series of family relocations, is in danger of emptying herself in a similar way.

In spiritual terms, it's also easy to reject the idea that men are by nature closer to the Divine (or, put another way, more filled with soul) as an outmoded belief. But think again. How many of the world's religions still give special responsibilities and privileges to men, while assigning women to veiled, 'protected' or second-class status? Even today, in many traditional Western marriage ceremonies, a man promises to 'love and protect', while a woman vows to 'serve and obey'. Consider where you have located your soul, the Little Mermaid warns. Make sure your own life is soul-filled, instead of relying on something or someone outside yourself to provide a satisfying fullness of being.

The Little Mermaid gives up her personal power in other ways that are familiar to women today. Believing that it's necessary to suffer, in order to be beautiful in someone else's eyes, is a kind of disempowerment that is very recognizable. In a way, conforming to a standard of beauty dictated by someone else – a fashion magazine, a boyfriend, your mother – is another version of soul loss. The

next time you dress in a way that is uncomfortable for you personally, but feels necessary in order to win the approval of others, think of the Little Mermaid with eight big oysters stuck onto her tail!

Loss of Self

On one level, of course, the Little Mermaid takes her quest for beauty further than most women would go today. She agrees not only to suffer, but actually to become a cripple, unable to walk without pain, for the sake of being desirable to the Prince. But in these days of liposuction, botox injections, facelifts and extreme makeovers, perhaps the Sea Witch's magic potion is not so far from reality after all. The two-edged sword that goes through the Little Mermaid's body when she drinks the potion symbolizes today's double threat to a woman's healthy sense of self, as posed by the plastic-surgeon's scalpel and the body hatred that motivates a woman to submit to it.

The loss of self that seems most terrible to the Little Mermaid is giving up her beautiful voice. Interestingly, this detail is not eliminated from the otherwise sanitized film version of the story. It

seems that a contemporary audience can still identify with the Little Mermaid's willingness to silence herself for the sake of winning the man she loves. Women who choose to bite their tongue rather than risk an argument with a partner have made a similar choice. But a good figure and nice moves on the dance floor are a poor substitute for the ability to speak your own truth, as the Little Mermaid discovers.

Loss of Female Sexuality

The final sacrifice that the Little Mermaid makes is one that she never intended – the loss of her womanly sexual power. Though the Prince loves her, he treats her like a child or a friend, not like a potential marriage partner. He dresses her as his page – in other words, in boy's clothes – and takes her horseback riding and mountain climbing. As a final indignity, though he clearly does not mean it as such, he allows her to sleep on a velvet cushion outside his door.

This reversal of the traditional image of the mermaid as seductive and powerfully sexual can be traced in part to Andersen's

own psychology and life story. He never married, and biographers say that his closest emotional attachments were with men. Today he might have come out of the closet and written an entirely different kind of fairy tale. However, the story he did write carries a potent message about the dangers of sublimation – channelling one's erotic energies into more socially acceptable activities.

Women sublimate their sexual desire in a number of ways: they redirect it into a high-powered professional career or a full-time commitment to creative work, putting off a husband and children for some future time that may never arrive. They channel it into 24-hour mothering, leaving little time or energy for keeping the fires of romance burning in their marriage. They focus it on volunteer work or on caring for elderly relatives, believing that unconditional service to others is the highest good, even when it leaves them feeling burned out and resentful. They substitute intimate friendships with women or with men who are not sexually

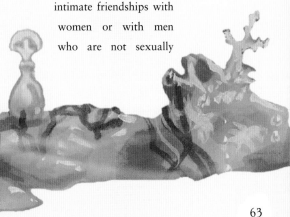

available – a married work colleague, a gay friend – for a genuine partner. If any of these life stories ring true for you, bring to mind the image of the Little Mermaid holding the wedding train of the Prince's bride and consider what you might do to rewrite your own story.

Women also hold back from sexual intimacy because they fear its transformative power. Given Andersen's ambivalence about sex, the unpleasant erotic imagery that surrounds the Sea Witch makes sense. It also seems appropriate for the adolescent Little Mermaid to find the slimy polyps and fat water snakes frightening. But when she has passed these trials and is with the Prince, the Little Mermaid is unable to grow up and relate to

him as a woman, perhaps because adult sexuality feels like death to her – remember the little mermaid the polyps have strangled? Women who are still little girls sexually have amputated their erotic nature – and their mermaid tails – in a similar way.

The True Nature of Love

Neither the ending of Andersen's story nor the feel-good conclusion of the film offers a satisfying resolution to the questions the story raises about the true nature of love. In the film, the Little Mermaid, with her animal helpers, breaks the spell that has the Prince marrying a disguised Sea Witch, gets back her voice and thwarts the Sea Witch's scheme to rule the ocean. After the Sea Witch dies horribly, the Sea King turns the Little Mermaid into a human girl who marries the Prince so that she can be forever part of his world. Though on the surface everyone is happy, the Little Mermaid sails off into her new life leaving her true nature behind.

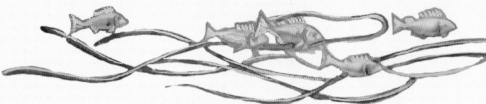

In Andersen's story, the Little Mermaid also seems to get her wish. Because she has suffered and endured, she can earn a human soul by three hundred years of selfless good works. Though Andersen clearly intended the Little Mermaid's transition to the spiritual realm to be a happy ending, he has consigned his heroine to a kind of purgatory – to salvation through caring for others, rather than through satisfying her natural and appropriate desires.

Though it's right in a spiritual sense that the truest kind of love arises from a wish to relieve the suffering of a loved person and to make that person happy, it's also essential for a woman to love herself enough to make her own life personally fulfilling. The Little Mermaid's tears at the end of the story seem to have two meanings. They are tears of joy that her wish for spiritual immortality can be achieved, but they also remind you how sad it is that women often settle for second best in life, rather than winning the loving relationship they desire and deserve.

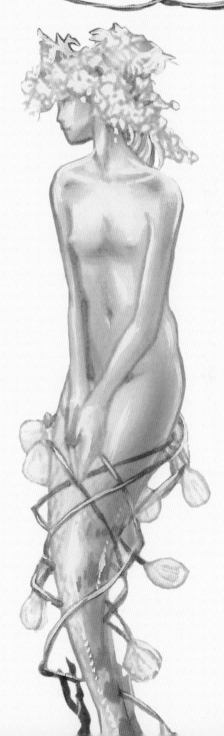

A String of Pearls

In this exercise you will map some of the whirlpools and submerged rocks that threaten the smooth sailing of your love relationships. Along the way you will also chart your underlying assumptions about the nature of love, and consider how you might want to alter the course you are following.

Perhaps you have noticed that your love relationships follow a pattern. You might think of each relationship as a pearl on the string of pearls that is your love life so far. Your task is to examine each pearl in order to appreciate its unique qualities, and to pay attention to the ways your pearls are strung together.

* * *

HERE'S WHAT TO DO

1 **Sit comfortably,** close your eyes and take several deep breaths, focusing your attention on the rise and fall of your abdomen as you breathe, until you feel yourself to be centred and relaxed.

2 **Invite an image to arise** in your mind of someone you have loved at some point in your life. Bring this person vividly to life in your mind, remembering his face, his way of walking and speaking, the clothes he wore, his favourite foods and activities. Put yourself into the scene and recall how it was to spend time with him, paying particular attention to your feelings. Appreciate as fully as you can everything that was wonderful about this relationship, but also allow yourself to remember everything about it that was challenging or caused you pain.

3 **When you feel** that your examination of this pearl has reached a natural ending, lay it aside and return your attention to your breath.

4 **When you are centred again,** invite the image to arise in your mind of someone else you have loved at some other point in your life, either earlier than the first pearl or later. Again, bring the details of the relationship and your feelings about it (both positive and negative) vividly to mind. When your appreciation of this pearl has reached a natural ending, take a moment to note any similarities or differences between this relationship and the first one you examined. It's not necessary to reach any conclusions about these experiences. Simply note them down and then return your attention to your breath.

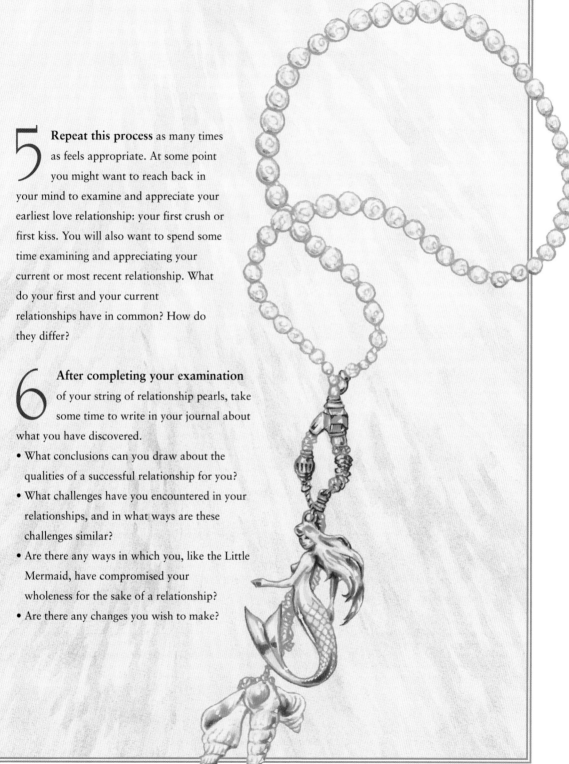

5 **Repeat this process** as many times as feels appropriate. At some point you might want to reach back in your mind to examine and appreciate your earliest love relationship: your first crush or first kiss. You will also want to spend some time examining and appreciating your current or most recent relationship. What do your first and your current relationships have in common? How do they differ?

6 **After completing your examination** of your string of relationship pearls, take some time to write in your journal about what you have discovered.

- What conclusions can you draw about the qualities of a successful relationship for you?
- What challenges have you encountered in your relationships, and in what ways are these challenges similar?
- Are there any ways in which you, like the Little Mermaid, have compromised your wholeness for the sake of a relationship?
- Are there any changes you wish to make?

Making a Relationship Treasure Map

This exercise invites you to create a treasure map, an actual physical picture of the relationship you want – the happy ending to your personal fairy tale. The idea behind making the map is that what you believe in, expect or ask for helps to create the conditions in which your dream can come true.

For this exercise you will need a large sheet of heavy paper or poster board, scissors, glue, drawing materials such as paints, markers or coloured pencils, and a selection of magazines, cards, letters, photographs and other items you can cut up to make a collage. You will also need some paper or your journal.

✳ ✳ ✳

HERE'S WHAT TO DO

1 **Write a series of short sentences** on a piece of paper or in your journal that describe your vision of a deeply satisfying love relationship. Include qualities that are present in your current relationship, as well as those that you wish were there. If you are not in a relationship now, describe the relationship you would most like to have. For instance:

- We're crazy about dogs.
- We enjoy travelling together.
- We are caring parents.
- We enjoy working together in our beautiful garden.
- We make love often.

2 **Create a collage** – using your art supplies as well as pictures and words cut out of magazines and other sources, pasted on your heavy paper or poster board – that shows your ideal relationship as if it already exists. Refer to the list of statements you have written above as a guide to what to include. For instance, include photos from a magazine of a couple playing in the park with their dogs, sipping wine in a picturesque restaurant on a Greek island, taking their children to the zoo, gardening together, or cuddling in bed. It's not necessary to explain how any of these things are going to come about. Your map is a picture of the treasure you are seeking, not the steps you have to take to find it.

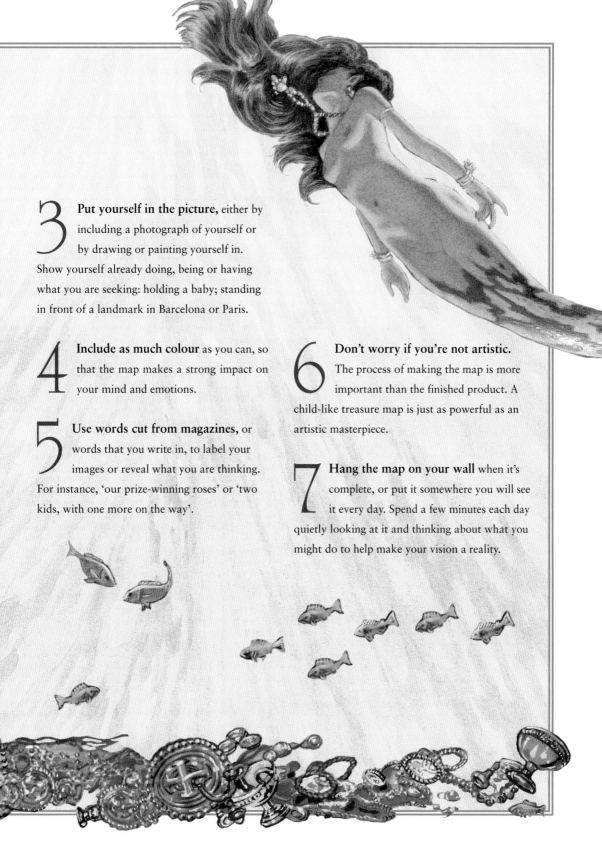

3 **Put yourself in the picture,** either by including a photograph of yourself or by drawing or painting yourself in. Show yourself already doing, being or having what you are seeking: holding a baby; standing in front of a landmark in Barcelona or Paris.

4 **Include as much colour** as you can, so that the map makes a strong impact on your mind and emotions.

5 **Use words cut from magazines,** or words that you write in, to label your images or reveal what you are thinking. For instance, 'our prize-winning roses' or 'two kids, with one more on the way'.

6 **Don't worry if you're not artistic.** The process of making the map is more important than the finished product. A child-like treasure map is just as powerful as an artistic masterpiece.

7 **Hang the map on your wall** when it's complete, or put it somewhere you will see it every day. Spend a few minutes each day quietly looking at it and thinking about what you might do to help make your vision a reality.

CHAPTER 5
THE SIREN

* * *

O, train me not, sweet mermaid, with thy note,

To drown me in thy sister's flood of tears.

Sing, siren, for thyself, and I will dote.

Spread o'er the silver waves thy golden hairs,

And as a bed I'll take them and there lie;

And in that glorious supposition think

He gains by death that hath such means to die.

WILLIAM SHAKESPEARE (1564–1616), THE COMEDY OF ERRORS

Like Antipholus of Syracuse, who speaks these words in Shakespeare's *The Comedy of Errors*, men have always been attracted to sexy, siren-like women. Though they know that sirens are deadly, danger is part of their allure. 'What a way to go!' is a modern version of the last line of Antipholus' poetic come-on to the beautiful Luciana. But the lure of the siren is more than sex; it is the sometimes irresistible call to knowing and having it all.

Where did the association of the siren with danger and death come from? How can women reclaim the siren as an image of feminine power? And how can she teach you to use your own sexuality wisely?

To answer these questions, this chapter tells the tale of the original Sirens taken from Homer's *Odyssey*, and an English folktale about a siren who uses her wiles to take revenge on a man who has mistreated a human woman. These stories illustrate destructive and constructive ways of using siren skills. You will also learn to recognize the sirens you encounter in your everyday world and to explore the tradition of the temptress as teacher – the loftiest use of a woman's seductive powers. Exercises help you consider your own responses to the siren's song and explore the role the siren plays in your personality.

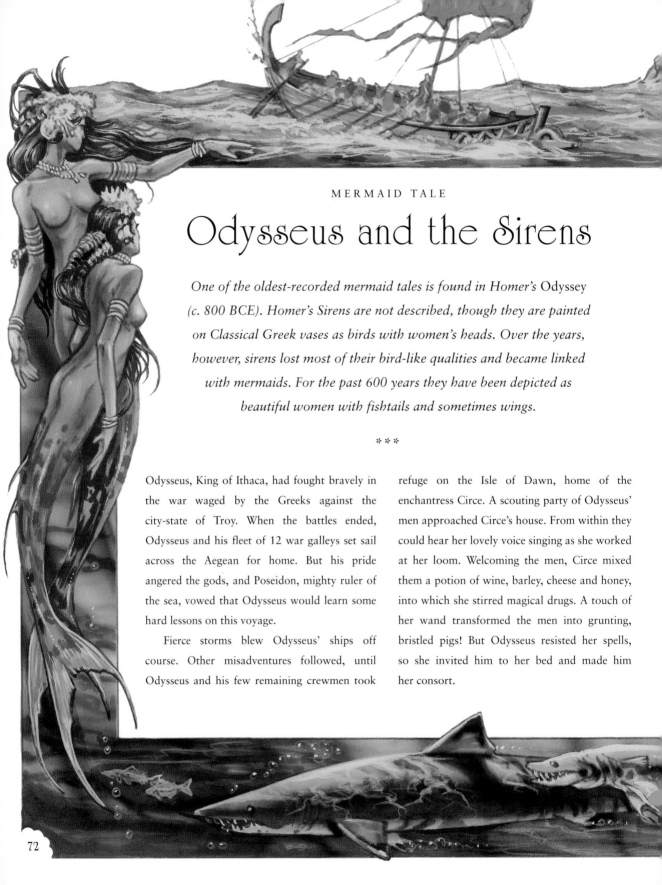

Odysseus and the Sirens

One of the oldest-recorded mermaid tales is found in Homer's Odyssey
*(c. 800 BCE). Homer's Sirens are not described, though they are painted
on Classical Greek vases as birds with women's heads. Over the years,
however, sirens lost most of their bird-like qualities and became linked
with mermaids. For the past 600 years they have been depicted as
beautiful women with fishtails and sometimes wings.*

* * *

Odysseus, King of Ithaca, had fought bravely in the war waged by the Greeks against the city-state of Troy. When the battles ended, Odysseus and his fleet of 12 war galleys set sail across the Aegean for home. But his pride angered the gods, and Poseidon, mighty ruler of the sea, vowed that Odysseus would learn some hard lessons on this voyage.

Fierce storms blew Odysseus' ships off course. Other misadventures followed, until Odysseus and his few remaining crewmen took refuge on the Isle of Dawn, home of the enchantress Circe. A scouting party of Odysseus' men approached Circe's house. From within they could hear her lovely voice singing as she worked at her loom. Welcoming the men, Circe mixed them a potion of wine, barley, cheese and honey, into which she stirred magical drugs. A touch of her wand transformed the men into grunting, bristled pigs! But Odysseus resisted her spells, so she invited him to her bed and made him her consort.

When, after long persuasion and further adventures under Circe's direction, Odysseus convinced the enchantress to allow him and his men to leave, Circe took him on one side to warn him of the dangers he would pass on the next part of his voyage.

'First, you will encounter the Sirens,' she said, 'beautiful creatures who seduce men with honey-sweet music. Whoever hears the Sirens' song never returns to his wife and children, but remains for ever on their island among the heaps of bones of men they have captivated.'

'What must I do?' Odysseus asked.

'Soften some beeswax in your hands and stuff it into the ears of your crewmen so that none of them can listen. But if you are keen to hear the music, command your sailors to lash you to the mast. Should you beg them to release you, make sure you have ordered them to bind you tighter still. Only then can you safely listen.'

At dawn, with a fair wind, Odysseus and his men set sail. Odysseus told his crew about Circe's warning and gave his orders. When the Sirens' isle came into view, the wind died away and the waves became still. Odysseus cut a large round of wax into bits with his sword and plugged his comrades' ears. Then he stood upright against the mast, to which his crewmen lashed him securely hand and foot.

As the sailors rowed through the becalmed seas, the Sirens sang. 'Odysseus, mighty hero, great glory of the Greeks, listen to our song. Bliss it brings, but wisdom, too, for we know all that has happened and all that is to come. Come, let us teach you.'

Hearing this, Odysseus longed to hear more, and with his eyes he begged his men to free him. But instead they bound him even more tightly and rowed on, until the seductive music was safely behind them.

Mermaid Seduction

The mermaid as siren is a femme fatale – a seductive woman who uses her wiles to ensnare or entangle others. The term 'siren' actually comes from a Greek word that means cord or rope. Sirens use their beauty, their sexuality and their honeyed voices to rope others in.

* * *

Sirens are not always classically beautiful, but they exude an unmistakable sexuality. Though you might think that you're most likely to see a contemporary siren prowling the edge of the dance floor or perched provocatively on a pub stool, look around. Perhaps there's a perfectly pedicured and coiffed siren sitting at the next desk in your office, or watering her flowers down the street from your house in jeans that are just slightly too tight!

Consciously using your sexuality as a lure is often appropriate. After all, flirting – a siren skill – is how we generally attract our mates. Sadly, sirens sometimes have trouble banking down their seductive fires when a less provocative approach is more appropriate. Moreover, sirens are often equally seductive towards people of either sex, as they have discovered that magnetizing people with their charm is an effective means of getting their way. Women whose voices drop to a silky purr when they are trying to get you to do what they want are actually singing a siren song.

Male Responses to the Sirens' Song

Men react to the siren song in different ways. Some, like Odysseus' mariners, stuff their ears with beeswax so that they are impervious to its enticement. If you've ever tried to attract the attention of a man whose nose is always buried in the sports pages or who's too busy questing through cyberspace to return your phone calls or answer your emails, then you've encountered the modern equivalent of beeswax.

Braver men, like Odysseus, may wish to hear the siren's song because they appreciate its beauty, but lash themselves to the mast so that they can't fall under its spell. Chronic workaholics fall into this category, as do men who fill their days with golf dates, poker nights and service-club meetings. At some level these men know that heeding the siren's song will change their lives, and they fear change most of all.

The siren's song is always a call to transformation. In Classical Greece, the call of the siren was equated with wisdom – even with the ability to foretell the future. The philosopher Plato equated the siren's song with the music of the spheres: the celestial harmonies created by the stars moving through the heavens in their circular dance. Hearing the music of the spheres conferred God-like understanding of the patterns of existence.

Though the quest for such ultimate knowledge can be dangerous, it is in fact what draws us to venture beyond the comfort zone of what we already know. It seduced early sailors into exploring the unknown waters beyond the charted horizon. It calls us today to a passion for going deeper – in our studies, our relationships, our spirituality.

Personifying wisdom as an enticingly beautiful goddess or an irresistibly sexy siren – as happens in many myths – points to the loftiest use of seduction. Desire is, after all, a powerful motivating force, and focusing the considerable energy of sexuality on the quest for personal, creative and spiritual growth can be transformative for both sirens and their partners.

The Temptress as Teacher

The siren belongs to an ancient and powerful tradition of the temptress as teacher. Though the promise of sexual pleasure is her primary lure, she also attracts men with the enticement of profound understanding. To become the consort of a wisdom goddess transforms and deepens a man, as Odysseus discovers when he becomes Circe's lover. The man who sets sail from Circe's island is more mindful, humble and mature than the brash war hero who sailed from Troy years earlier.

* * *

Circe herself has many siren-like qualities. Her lovely singing voice and the loom on which she combs her weaving are reminiscent of mermaids. Moreover, under her direction, Odysseus is sent to visit Hades, the underworld realm of the dead, from which he returns with a new understanding of his character and knowledge of his destiny. Significantly, Odysseus' important teachers in the underworld are also women, including his own mother (who has died of grief during his long absence) and the mothers of other famous heroes. Visiting the underworld is like dying, and the wise women Odysseus meets in Hades are like sirens, in that a man must descend into death in order to learn from them.

This ancient understanding of the siren as a teacher differs sharply from the later and more familiar view. To early Christians, the siren was a symbol of the dangers of lust and the base desires that could lure men to stray from the narrow path of virtue. In medieval Europe, carvings of sirens appeared frequently in churches on bench ends and the capitals of pillars to warn the faithful, and sirens were pictured in early books to illustrate the temptations of the flesh. The message of the Church was clear: woman is a temptress who can draw a man down to perdition. 'Sail past the song; it works death,' exhorted Church father Clement of Alexandria in the third century CE.

The Siren as Wise Woman

Women, however, have always understood that sirens and other powerfully sexual goddess figures are holders of traditional feminine wisdom. Like sirens, the Great Mother goddesses of the ancient world – Ishtar and Innana in the Middle East, Aphrodite in Greece – were alternately cruel and kind. Their consorts were also initiates into their mysteries, and the rites of fertility they enacted often ended with the consort's death.

The European tradition is similar. In Brittany, mermaids are called 'morgens' to recall their descent from Morgan Le Fay, the wise-woman sorceress of the Arthurian legends. When St Patrick brought Christianity to Ireland, tradition has it that the pagan wise women he banished were transformed into mermaids. Honouring the siren reminds you that your woman's body and your sexuality are sacred. Choose carefully the consorts you invite to your bed and initiate into your mysteries!

As teachers and wise women, sirens are also the guardians of human women, as you will discover in the story 'The Mermaid's Revenge' (see pages 78–79). Though the mermaid in this tale behaves like a typical siren, seducing a man and bearing him down to a watery grave, she does so to avenge his cruelty to a human girl who she has been protecting.

The Mermaid's Revenge

This folktale comes from Cornwall. Many versions are told on the Lizard peninsula, near the coves around Land's End and along the north coast near the Pool of Perran, which is reputed to be a favourite haunt of mermaids.

* * *

A farmer and his wife once lived in a modest cottage on the north coast of Cornwall. Their joy was their daughter Selina, whose apple cheeks and midnight eyes were much admired. The village wise women said that Selina's great beauty had a mysterious source. At the fire on winter evenings they told the tale.

'When Selina was a babe,' the gossips said, 'her mother was out walking with her near the Pool of Perran. Suddenly, the child jumped from her arms into the water. When she floated to the surface, right as rain, she was more bright and beautiful than ever.'

As she grew, Selina's favourite pastime was walking along the seashore. On one such walk,

in her eighteenth year, a handsome young soldier by the name of Walter Trewoofe rode past on his fine horse. Taken by the girl's beauty, Walter asked his uncle, a wealthy squire he was visiting, who she was.

'A poor farmer's daughter,' the squire replied. 'Not for the likes of you.'

But Walter was smitten and could not be dissuaded. Soon he and Selina were walking together along the beach. For her part, Selina was much taken by the young man's dash and style and soon gave him her trust, her virginity and her innocent heart.

One evening, as the pair lay on the shore in each other's arms, an old fisherman saw a strange

sight. A mermaid rose from the waves quite near the couple and then disappeared with an angry slap of her tail. 'It's as if the seamaid was watching out for the girl,' he told his wife when he got home.

Having won the girl, Walter – who was a bit of a cad, if the truth be told – grew tired of her. One day, without a word to her, he rode out of Cornwall and returned to his regiment. Selina was heartbroken. She no longer found pleasure in strolling along the beach. As the babe in her belly grew, she became despondent and her life force faded, until one dark day she died of grief.

That spring, the rains were late and the crops failed. Horses grew lame and calves died. It was as if all of nature was mourning Selina's death. In the summer Walter returned to visit his uncle. One night after drinking some wine, he was walking along the beach when he heard a woman's voice singing a haunting and beautiful song. He followed the sound and came to a cavern where a beautiful woman sat singing. His heart thumped madly, for she had Selina's apple cheeks and midnight eyes.

'Come sit beside me, Walter,' she said.

Walter could not say no. But when he kissed the mysterious beauty, he knew she was not Selina.

'Kiss a maiden and destroy her,' the seamaid whispered as she wrapped her arms tightly around Walter's neck. 'Kiss a seamaid and you are hers for ever,' she cried as she bore Walter down to his death beneath the waves.

The Siren's Song

The siren's song may come to you as an irresistible call to pleasure – a vacation trip that you can't afford, an impractical red sports car, a dinner invitation from an attractive man you know will break your heart. Or your siren's song may be the delight of knowing everything there is to know – conversational Italian, crochet for beginners, salsa dancing – luring you into signing up for too many workshops and buying too many books. Alternatively, as happened to Odysseus, your sirens may flatter you as a way of getting you to do what they want. 'You're always so helpful!' your neighbour exclaims, before asking you to babysit for the third time this month.

Seductions like these are not always a problem, as they can motivate you to venture further and delve deeper. Difficulties arise only when you fail to take the necessary precautions or to set appropriate limits. Here are some ways to enjoy your sirens' music without lashing yourself to the mast. For this exercise you will need your journal or some paper and a pen.

* * *

HERE'S WHAT TO DO

1 **List ten 'forbidden pleasures',** with your inner siren's help: things you adore, but don't often allow yourself to indulge in: eating a box of chocolates; spending the whole day in bed; calling a friend in South Africa and talking for as long as you want. Then brainstorm some creative ways to enjoy these pleasures: buy a box of individually wrapped chocolates and eat one each day until the box is empty; send the kids to your mother when your partner is out of town and spend the day in bed; pack a lunch instead of eating out, until you've saved enough to cover the phone bill.

2 **List ten crazy things** you would love to try. If it helps to get you started, write at the top of the page: 'I know it sounds crazy, but I would like to try ...' and then list the things your inner siren whispers: scuba diving; living on an island; motorcycling; colouring your hair blonde. Circle one item that calls to you right now, then brainstorm safe ways you could try it: read a book about scuba diving; call Tony and ask him about his Caribbean diving trip; plan a summer holiday to a resort that offers scuba lessons.

3 **List ten subjects** you would like to learn more about: calligraphy, Feng Shui decorating, ice skating, Chinese wok cooking. Think carefully about how much time and money you can responsibly devote; then choose one and sign up.

4 **List ten compliments** or instances of encouragement from others that have helped you to feel good about your accomplishments. If you are stuck, travel back through your memories and bring to mind a favourite teacher, an old boyfriend, your best friend from childhood. Be as specific as you can in recalling what this person said or did. On days when you need help in motivating yourself to do something you've been avoiding, read the list and let a bit of healthy self-flattery get you going.

Innocent, Destroyer and Protector

The characters in myths and folktales are so powerful and interesting because they often embody inner parts of the human personality. For instance, it's easy to recognize the three characters in 'The Mermaid's Revenge' (see pages 78–79)– Selina, Walter and the siren – as representing the *innocent*, the *destroyer* and the *protector*. This exercise helps you explore these aspects of your own nature. After you have considered how the innocent, the destroyer and the protector have been expressed in your life, you will enjoy portraying what you have discovered in some creative way, such as writing about it in your journal or making a drawing or collage.

* * *

HERE'S WHAT TO DO

Explore the following three aspects of yourself:

• **The innocent** is the part of you that trusts life and always thinks the best of other people. She keeps the faith and hopes for the best. When you look for the innocent in yourself, it's often easiest to find it in the child you were. But you will also find your inner innocent in the child-like parts of your adult self: your ability to be optimistic, loyal and forward-looking. The innocent's greatest fear is abandonment, and her greatest challenge is learning discernment – how to use intelligence and judgement to decide who should be feared and who can be trusted.

Consider: what does your inner innocent look like? How does she act? Where and how did you embody the innocent in the past? Where and how do you embody her today? Is there anything you wish you could change about the way the innocent part of you expresses itself?

• **The destroyer** is the part that is the inner cause of your suffering. She can be embodied in any of your self-destructive habits and behaviours, including physical addictions (such as smoking, drinking or disordered eating) and emotional addictions (such as abusive relationships). But you will also find the destroyer in the ways you react to external life events that cause you to

suffer. She intensifies your suffering when you are afraid to let go and allow change to happen. Her challenge is accepting life's inevitable losses and disappointments.

Consider: what does your inner destroyer look like? How does she act? Where and how did you embody the destroyer in the past? Where and how do you embody the destroyer today? Is there anything you wish you could change about the way the destructive part of you expresses itself?

Consider: what does your inner protector look like? How does she act? Where and how did you embody the protector in the past? Where and how do you embody the protector today? Is there anything you wish you could change about the way the protective part of you expresses itself?

- **The protector** is the part of you that looks out for you and has your best interests at heart. She takes you to the doctor for a check-up, motivates you to eat healthy foods and get enough exercise, and warns you to steer clear of potentially dangerous situations and hurtful people. To keep your protector on alert, you must fearlessly cut through mental confusion so that you can hear the inner intuitive voice that is trying to keep you safe. Your protector's challenge is being strong and assertive in your defence, without making you lose your cool.

CHAPTER 6
LAND AND SEA

* * *

'Twas Friday morn when we set sail,

And we had not got far from land,

When the Captain, he spied a lovely
mermaid,

With a comb and a glass in her hand.

Chorus: Oh the ocean waves may roll,

And the stormy winds may blow,

While we poor sailors go skipping aloft

And the land lubbers lay down below,
below, below

And the land lubbers lay down below.

Then up spoke the Captain of our
gallant ship,

And a jolly old Captain was he;

'I have a wife in Salem town,

But tonight a widow she will be.'

CHORUS

Then up spoke the Cook of our
gallant ship,

And a greasy old Cook was he;

'I care more for my kettles and my pots,

Than I do for the roaring of the sea.'

CHORUS

Then up spoke the Cabin-boy of our
gallant ship,

And a dirty little brat was he;

'I have friends in Boston town

That don't care a ha'penny for me.'

CHORUS

Then three times 'round went our
gallant ship,

And three times 'round went she,

And the third time that she went 'round

She sank to the bottom of the sea.

FRANCIS J. CHILD (1825–1896), 'THE MERMAID'

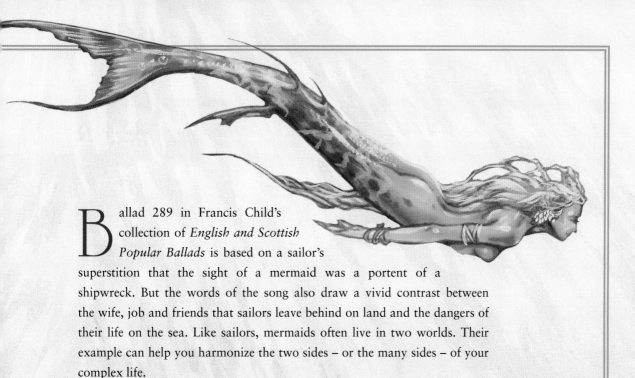

Ballad 289 in Francis Child's collection of *English and Scottish Popular Ballads* is based on a sailor's superstition that the sight of a mermaid was a portent of a shipwreck. But the words of the song also draw a vivid contrast between the wife, job and friends that sailors leave behind on land and the dangers of their life on the sea. Like sailors, mermaids often live in two worlds. Their example can help you harmonize the two sides – or the many sides – of your complex life.

What can mermaids teach you about how to balance a divided life? How can you more easily reconcile the conflicting demands of work and play, career and family, friends and lovers, material and spiritual life?

To answer these questions, this chapter presents two lovely stories from indigenous cultures. From the New Zealand Maoris comes the story of the sea maiden Pania, who nearly succeeds in living happily on both land and sea. From the Native Americans of eastern Canada comes the tale of Menana, who leaves the sea behind completely to marry the young chief she loves. Both stories carry powerful messages about what a woman needs in order to feel balanced and whole. Exercises help you harmonize the four elements of your body, and guide you through a powerful art-therapy process that can help you release tensions and resolve life conflicts.

Pania of the Reef

A bronze statue of Pania sits on the Marine Parade sea front in Napier on the east coast of New Zealand's North Island. Like the famous statue of the Little Mermaid in Copenhagen harbour, it is a reminder of how difficult it is for a mermaid to live in two worlds.

* * *

When the sun was high, Pania, a beautiful sea maiden, swam with the creatures of the reef. But when the sun sank into the sea, she would swim up a fresh-water stream that ran into the bay and would hide among the flax bushes at the foot of the cliff.

Each evening Karitoki, the handsome son of a Maori chief, came to drink from the sweet waters of the stream. For many weeks Pania watched him from her hiding place, until one evening, whispering an ancient love spell, she stepped out from behind the bushes.

Seeing her, Karitoki fell instantly in love. 'Be my wife,' he said, taking her hand.

'Be my husband,' Pania replied. And so, according to Maori custom, they were married.

After dark, Karitoki took Pania to his *whare* (house). There they rested side by side through the long, sweet hours of night. At dawn Pania arose. 'Where are you going, my wife?' Karitoki asked, his voice heavy with sleep.

'I hear my siren sisters calling and must go to them,' Pania replied. 'I am a creature of the sea and cannot live solely on land. Meet me at sunset at the foot of the cliff this night and all the nights to come, and I can be your wife.'

Pania kept her word. Each evening she met Karitoki and went with him to his *whare*. Each

morning she returned to the reef. Even after Pania had given birth to a fine baby boy, she wrapped the baby snugly each morning and took him with her to the reef.

'But he is my son, too,' Karitoki complained. 'He should belong to the land as well.'

'Our son is a creature of the sea,' Pania said as she bundled the baby up to leave.

Karitoki went to the *kaumatua* (wise elder) to ask his advice.

'A sea creature who eats the cooked food of the land cannot return to the sea,' the *kaumatua* said. 'At night when your wife and son are fast asleep in your *whare*, slip a morsel of stewed taro into their mouths.'

That night Karitoki took a tiny piece of taro and put it into Pania's mouth. As he was about to put a piece into the baby's mouth, a *morepork* (owl) called a loud warning, and Pania awoke.

Snatching up the child, Pania ran to the sea and dived into the reef. As Karitoki waded into the surf, he saw Pania release the child into the waves, where he became *mango*, the shark, who guards the reef to this day.

Pania herself sank into the sea, never again to be seen on land. But some people say that they can see her, deep in the waters of the reef, her arms outstretched. But whether she is imploring Karitoki to explain his betrayal, or telling him how much she misses him, is impossible to say.

87

Living in Two Worlds

How many worlds do you live in? Given the complexity of most women's lives today,
you might find it a relief to inhabit only two worlds, like Pania. The competing
demands of career and family, work and play, friends and lovers, material and
spiritual life, require many women to perform a tricky balancing act, one that often
leaves them feeling stretched, stressed and anxious.

* * *

The story of Pania provides some clues that can help a modern woman keep her dual or multiple life in balance.

First, it's important to notice that Pania has no doubt about who she is. 'I am a creature of the sea,' she tells her husband. And although she clearly loves Karitoki, she just as clearly knows that she belongs to herself, not to him. Unlike Andersen's Little Mermaid (see pages 54–59), Pania has no wish to become a permanent part of her human husband's world. She knows what she needs to be happy. This self-knowledge makes her confident enough to assert her right to live according to her own nature, both on land and in the sea.

This lesson is underscored in an alternative version of the Pania story, which is also told in New Zealand. In this version, Pania wishes to remain on land because of her great love for Karitoki. Each day her siren sisters and sea mother call to her in their haunting voices, begging her to return to the sea. At first she cannot hear them, though Karitoki can. Then she ignores them, vowing to remain for ever with her human husband. Finally she is persuaded to swim out to meet her sisters and mother just this once. But when she does, the sea people surround her and pull her down into the caverns of the sea, so that she can never return to the human lands.

Hear your Inner Voice

To keep your life in balance, this alternative version seems to warn, listen to what your inner voice tells you, not to what others want you to do. When Pania wavers in her resolve, she loses the ability to choose her own destiny. If your inner voice tells you, for instance, that your wholeness requires you to spend an hour alone meditating every morning, to find a way to quit your job and go back to college, or to delay having children until you have met your career goals, don't let pressure from anyone – a sister, a mother, a friend, even a loving partner – persuade you to change your mind. Knowing clearly what you want to do is an essential step in figuring out how to accomplish it.

Finally, the story seems to say that wholeness does not require that a woman do only one thing to do it well. A fulfilling life can be composed of two sides, or of as many sides as a woman's true nature requires. Until her husband tries to trick her, Pania is happy alternating between the reef world and the human world. Women who spend time with their friends as well as their partner, who find creative ways to raise a family while advancing their career, or who make time in their schedules for creative or spiritual pursuits have learned Pania's lesson.

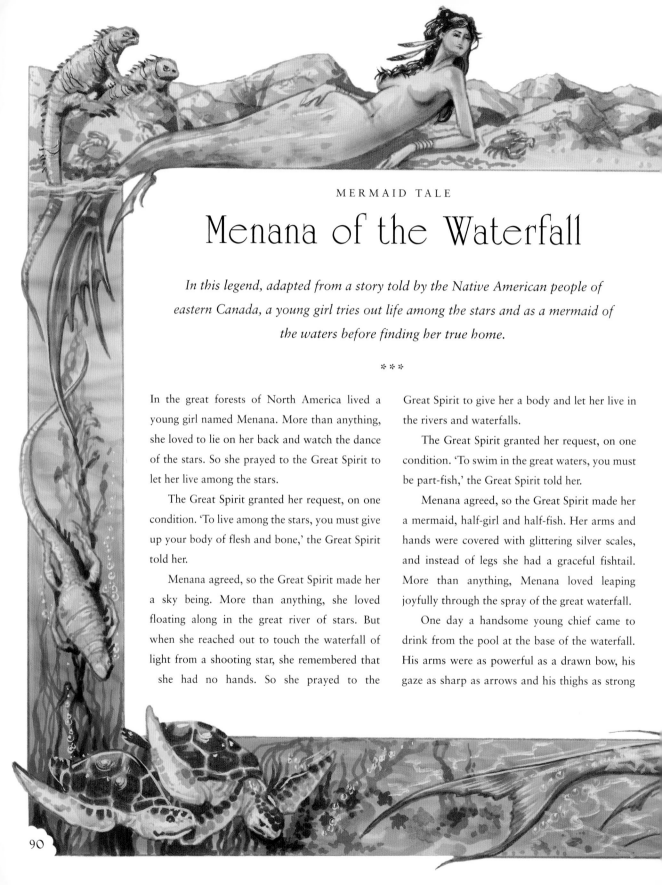

Menana of the Waterfall

*In this legend, adapted from a story told by the Native American people of
eastern Canada, a young girl tries out life among the stars and as a mermaid of
the waters before finding her true home.*

* * *

In the great forests of North America lived a young girl named Menana. More than anything, she loved to lie on her back and watch the dance of the stars. So she prayed to the Great Spirit to let her live among the stars.

The Great Spirit granted her request, on one condition. 'To live among the stars, you must give up your body of flesh and bone,' the Great Spirit told her.

Menana agreed, so the Great Spirit made her a sky being. More than anything, she loved floating along in the great river of stars. But when she reached out to touch the waterfall of light from a shooting star, she remembered that she had no hands. So she prayed to the

Great Spirit to give her a body and let her live in the rivers and waterfalls.

The Great Spirit granted her request, on one condition. 'To swim in the great waters, you must be part-fish,' the Great Spirit told her.

Menana agreed, so the Great Spirit made her a mermaid, half-girl and half-fish. Her arms and hands were covered with glittering silver scales, and instead of legs she had a graceful fishtail. More than anything, Menana loved leaping joyfully through the spray of the great waterfall.

One day a handsome young chief came to drink from the pool at the base of the waterfall. His arms were as powerful as a drawn bow, his gaze as sharp as arrows and his thighs as strong

as the trunks of young trees. In an instant Menana's heart was aflame with love.

So, once more, Menana prayed. 'Great Spirit, you have let me wander among the stars and swim in the rivers and waterfalls. But now, more than anything, I wish to be a human woman and marry the young chief I love with all my heart.'

The Great Spirit granted her request, on one condition. 'To be a human woman,' the Great Spirit told her, 'your untamed spirit must wander among the stars. Your laughter must be as playful as a creature of the waters. Your hands must weave the Earth's riches into a robe for a young chief to wear. Only then will you be a complete human being worthy of his love.'

Menana agreed. Emerging from the water on her new legs, she gathered mulberry bark and eagle feathers and plaited them into a beautiful robe. As she worked, her laughter was as playful as a leaping fish. At night, her spirit roamed the stars, filling her heart with moonlit dreams.

When the robe was finished, Menana waited near the pool at the base of the waterfall. When the young chief came to drink, she held out the robe. 'My heart is on fire for you,' she said. 'Tell me how I can win your love.'

'You already have,' the young chief replied, seeing the beauty of her spirit. 'Be my wife, and we will share life's joys and sorrows.'

And so they did.

Balancing the Four Elements

The legend of Menana invites you to consider what a woman needs in order to be whole and balanced. In Native American wisdom, a sense of wellbeing, and feeling at home in the world requires that humans align themselves with the qualities of the natural world, which are often linked to the four directions (north, south, east and west) and the four elements (air, earth, fire and water).

* * *

In the course of her brief story, Menana grows from a dreamy young girl to a complete and mature woman by embodying these four natural qualities. Her story suggests ways that you can achieve similar balance and wholeness.

As a young girl, perhaps you were a dreamer. Your spirit – linked in Native American wisdom with the north and the element of air – roamed among the dancing stars, delighted by an array of future possibilities. But as time went on, the constraints and responsibilities of a career and family may have weighed you down, and you came to feel that you have too much to do to waste time daydreaming. However, Menana's story reminds

you that to stay in balance, a woman needs to honour her air element by giving herself permission to follow her intuition, listen to the messages of her dreams and delight in the playful joy of dance and movement – whatever is needed to allow her untamed spirit to fly free.

The emotions are linked in Native American belief to the west and the element of water. When your emotions are not in balance, you may feel weepy and out of control, or buffeted by waves that alternately buoy you up and drop you into sadness or depression. In Menana's story, balancing the water element means becoming a mermaid, a creature who is completely at home in the watery

rhythms of the emotional world. Becoming a mermaid emotionally allows a woman to swim along with the currents of life while maintaining a sense of playfulness and joy. Rather than holding tight to preconceptions about the way things ought to be, she goes with the flow, so that she can enjoy the sparkling effervescence of new people and situations without losing her equilibrium.

The south and the element of earth symbolize the physical world. The earth is fruitful and productive, bringing forth everything that is green and growing: trees, grasses and flowers. Menana learns to honour her earth element by using her hands to weave the earth's riches into a beautiful robe by employing her art and creativity. To nurture your own wholeness, the story reminds you, make time in your life to be creative and to honour the bounty of the earth by cooking, gardening and spending time in nature.

The last element a woman needs is fire, which is linked to the east. For Menana, the fire of her love for the young chief is a source of life energy, like the radiant sun. It warms her from within and gives her the power to experience life's joys and sorrows without fear. Whether the love that sets your heart on fire is for another person, for a beloved animal or for some activity or hobby, Menana's story reminds you that loving someone or something is essential to enable a woman to be happy and whole.

Walking with the Four Elements

A wonderful way in which to balance your elements is by following the Native American practice of walking mindfully through the natural world. Choose a beautiful setting for your walk: the seashore, a wooded forest trail or a path through a city park or garden.

* * *

HERE'S WHAT TO DO

Consider the four elements and how you can harmonize them:

• **Air element** In nature, you experience the air element as a breeze or wind. In your body, it is your breath. Without air, nothing can move or change. In Native American wisdom the living breath of Grandfather Sky animates all life. Balancing your air element helps you to make essential changes. Focusing on your breath is also the easiest and most natural way to relax.

As you walk, pay attention to how the air feels on your face and exposed skin. Is it warm or cool? Is there any breeze or wind? What thoughts or feelings arise when you feel the air moving your hair or your clothes? Feel the rhythm of your inhalation and exhalation. Focus on your breathing as you walk, until you feel centred and relaxed.

• **Water element** You find the water element in the dew that clings to grass and leaves, in the ocean, lakes and streams, and in rain, snow and ice. In your body it is your blood and the fluids in and around your cells. To Native Americans, Grandmother Ocean is the womb of all life. Balancing your water element helps you wash away anxiety and calm your emotions.

Now turn your attention to any water that you see: a river or stream, the rain clouds overhead, a fountain or a well. Recall that your own body is mainly water, and how essential fluids are to your physical health. Consider the various ways in which your emotions

resemble nature's waters – storms of anger, waves of desire, deep wells of compassion. Invite your feelings to smooth themselves out like the peaceful surface of a lake.

• **Earth element** In nature, the earth element is every tree, flower, animal and insect, as well as the rocks and soil under your feet. In your body it is your organs, tissues and bones. Grandmother Earth protects and nurtures the growth of all living things: animals, plants and people. Walking on the earth keeps you grounded and helps you focus on the things you need to do.

Use all of your senses to experience the physical world as you walk – its colours and sounds, the softness of grass or earth, the scent of leaves or

flowers. Enjoy the sensation of being embodied, the beat of your heart, the pumping of your lungs, the expansion and contraction of your muscles as you walk.

• **Fire element** The sun above you represents the fire element, as does the molten core of the earth on which you are walking. Grandfather Fire provides the vital spark that creates light so that your eyes can see and your mind can envision. It also gives the warm heart at the centre of your being the energy to love.

Enjoy the sun's warmth on your body as you walk and observe the play of light that illumines everything you see. Bring to mind the people and things in your life that you love, and allow the inner radiance of your warm heart to lighten and energize your steps.

Balance your Many Worlds

This exercise can help you access and release the feeling of being stretched, stressed or troubled by the effort it takes to balance the many worlds you inhabit. You will need your journal or some paper and any drawing materials that you favour, such as coloured pencils, markers or crayons.

* * *

HERE'S WHAT TO DO

1 **Sit comfortably,** close your eyes and take several deep breaths, focusing your attention on the rise and fall of your abdomen as you breathe, until you feel centred and relaxed.

2 **Call to mind** a current situation in which conflicting demands have left you feeling stressed, anxious or frustrated. For instance, it could be that concern about your childcare arrangements is making you feel tense at the office. Set the intention that you will use this time to reflect on the situation and find a way to release your stress concerning it.

3 **Open your journal** or take a piece of paper and draw a vertical line down the centre of a page. On one side of the line, write about one side of the conflict; for instance, describe what you most enjoy and most dislike about staying at home with your children. On the other side of the line, write about the other half of the conflict; for instance, how concerns about your childcare impact upon your work life. Pay special attention to describing your feelings about each side of the conflict.

4 **Now close your eyes** and allow an image to arise in your mind that expresses the conflict you have described. What colours, shapes, forms or images best express your feelings? On a fresh page draw the image using your drawing materials. Keep in mind that you do not need to be an artist to benefit from this exercise. Even stick-figures or scribbles can help you access your feelings.

5 **Reflect on the image** you have drawn, once you have finished it. How do you feel when you look at it? What do the colours and shapes you have chosen reveal about your feelings? Describe your reaction to the drawing and what you have learned about the conflict by writing about it.

6 **Lay aside your drawing,** once this part of the exercise feels complete, then close your eyes and once again concentrate your attention on your breathing. Invite your mind to create a new image describing the situation that feels more positive or suggests a constructive way of resolving your conflicting feelings. Take a fresh page and draw the image. If a new image does not spring to mind, simply draw something that feels soothing.

7 **Reflect on the new picture,** once you have finished it. How do you feel when you look at it? What message does the drawing give you about what you might do to resolve your feelings concerning this situation?

8 **Describe what you have learned** from this exercise, about resolving the situation and balancing the competing demands in your life, by writing about it in your journal.

LAND AND SEA

97

CHAPTER 7

DIVING AND SURFACING

* * *

So sweet the hour, so calm the time,

I feel it more than half a crime,

When Nature sleeps and stars are mute,

To mar the silence ev'n with lute.

At rest on ocean's brilliant dyes

An image of Elysium lies:

Seven Pleiades entranced in Heaven,

Form in the deep another seven:

Endymion nodding from above

Sees in the sea a second love.

Within the valleys dim and brown,

And on the spectral mountain's crown,

The wearied light is dying down,

And earth, and stars, and sea, and sky

Are redolent of sleep, as I

Am redolent of thee and thine

Enthralling love, my Adeline.

But list, O list, – so soft and low

Thy lover's voice tonight shall flow,

That, scarce awake, thy soul shall deem

My words the music of a dream.

Thus, while no single sound too rude

Upon thy slumber shall intrude,

Our thoughts, our souls – O God above!

In every deed shall mingle, love.

EDGAR ALLAN POE (1809–1849), 'SERENADE'

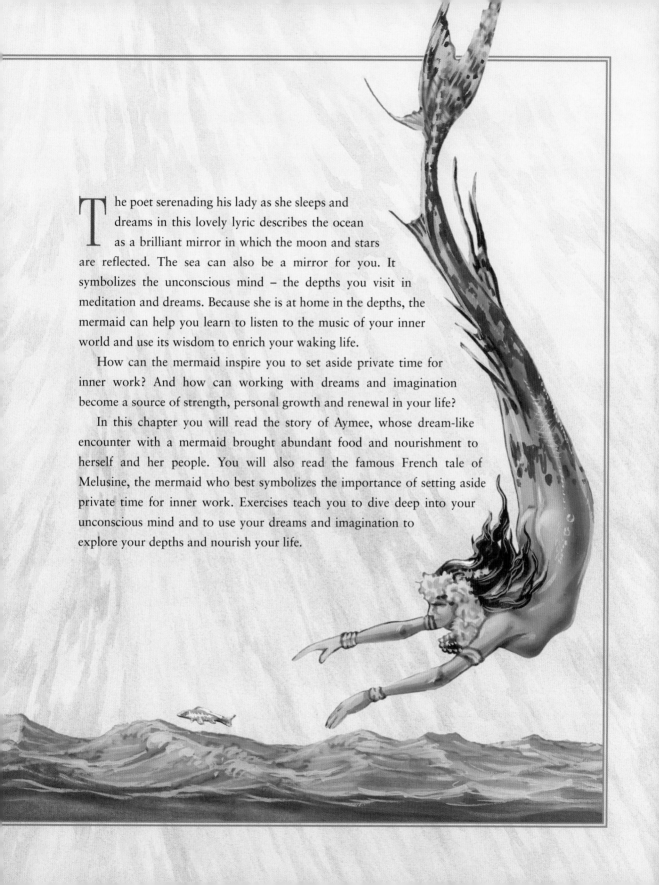

The poet serenading his lady as she sleeps and dreams in this lovely lyric describes the ocean as a brilliant mirror in which the moon and stars are reflected. The sea can also be a mirror for you. It symbolizes the unconscious mind – the depths you visit in meditation and dreams. Because she is at home in the depths, the mermaid can help you learn to listen to the music of your inner world and use its wisdom to enrich your waking life.

How can the mermaid inspire you to set aside private time for inner work? And how can working with dreams and imagination become a source of strength, personal growth and renewal in your life?

In this chapter you will read the story of Aymee, whose dream-like encounter with a mermaid brought abundant food and nourishment to herself and her people. You will also read the famous French tale of Melusine, the mermaid who best symbolizes the importance of setting aside private time for inner work. Exercises teach you to dive deep into your unconscious mind and to use your dreams and imagination to explore your depths and nourish your life.

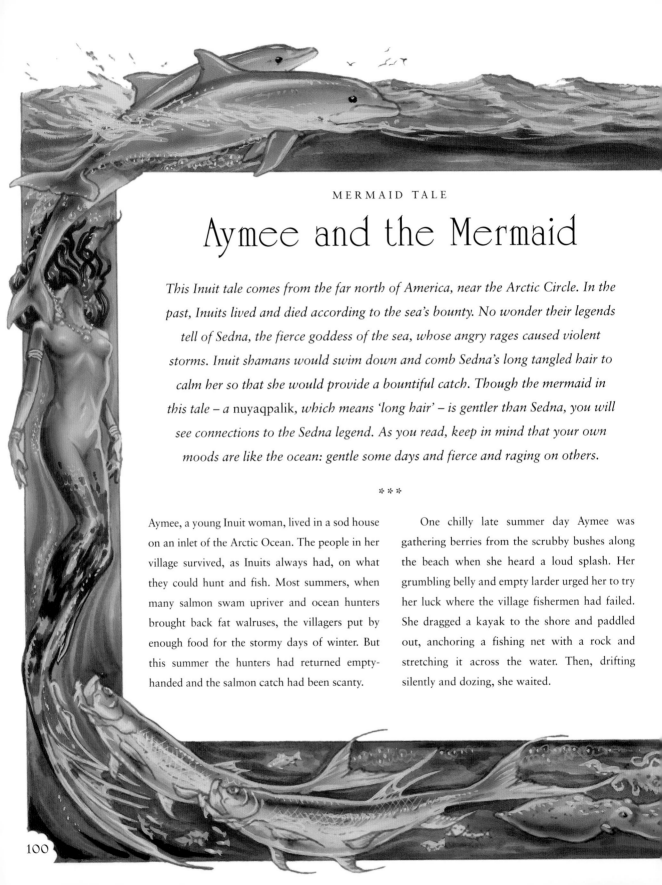

Aymee and the Mermaid

This Inuit tale comes from the far north of America, near the Arctic Circle. In the past, Inuits lived and died according to the sea's bounty. No wonder their legends tell of Sedna, the fierce goddess of the sea, whose angry rages caused violent storms. Inuit shamans would swim down and comb Sedna's long tangled hair to calm her so that she would provide a bountiful catch. Though the mermaid in this tale – a nuyaqpalik, *which means 'long hair' – is gentler than Sedna, you will see connections to the Sedna legend. As you read, keep in mind that your own moods are like the ocean: gentle some days and fierce and raging on others.*

* * *

Aymee, a young Inuit woman, lived in a sod house on an inlet of the Arctic Ocean. The people in her village survived, as Inuits always had, on what they could hunt and fish. Most summers, when many salmon swam upriver and ocean hunters brought back fat walruses, the villagers put by enough food for the stormy days of winter. But this summer the hunters had returned empty-handed and the salmon catch had been scanty.

One chilly late summer day Aymee was gathering berries from the scrubby bushes along the beach when she heard a loud splash. Her grumbling belly and empty larder urged her to try her luck where the village fishermen had failed. She dragged a kayak to the shore and paddled out, anchoring a fishing net with a rock and stretching it across the water. Then, drifting silently and dozing, she waited.

In her dream, Aymee saw herself swimming through the icy waters, her long tangled hair trailing behind her. Piece by piece, her body began to change.

First the fingers of her right hand dropped off and became a school of fat whitefish. Then the fingers of her left hand dropped off. One became a whale, one a seal, another a walrus, another a salmon. 'Yi-i-i-i,' Aymee howled and, with a start, woke up.

But the howl did not cease as she rubbed her eyes. Peering over the side of the kayak, she saw a fishtail covered with silver scales and then a head covered with long, black hair like Aymee's own! A mermaid's angry fingers gripped the side of the kayak, threatening to overturn it.

'Stop that,' Aymee cried bravely, though her voice shook. She pushed the *nuyaqpalik* away with her paddle. 'Your hair is caught in my net. You must be calm so that I can untangle it.'

As strand by strand Aymee separated the mermaid's long hair from the mesh, she spoke soothing words. 'I am a woman just like you. My people are hungry, so I set my net for whitefish. I did not mean to catch you.'

Though she said nothing, the mermaid seemed to understand. When the last tangle had been combed out by Aymee's patient fingers, the mermaid broke free and vanished with a slap of her tail.

The next morning when Aymee paddled out, her net was full and the inlet was swarming with fish. Village fishermen joined her and soon caught enough to last the winter.

Though Aymee never saw the mermaid from her kayak again, through the long winter nights the *nuyaqpalik* swam silently again and again through Aymee's dreams.

Inner Work

*Consciousness is like the mermaids' ocean. At the surface, ordinary things happen –
waves of thought tumble and roll, storms of feeling thunder and blow. The events of
daily life sail across the surface of consciousness like passing ships. But most of the
ocean's enormous energy is out of sight, below the surface.*

* * *

Deep in the sea of consciousness – in what depth psychologists (see page 8) call the unconscious mind – powerful forces are at work. The unconscious is like a vast undersea civilization, filled with images and symbols, characters and stories, emotions and memories. Psychologist Carl Jung compared consciousness to an iceberg. The part you're aware of – the conscious mind – is like the tip of the iceberg rising out of the Arctic Ocean. The unconscious mind – 95 per cent of the icy mass – is hiding beneath the waves.

You become aware of the contents of the unconscious when you feel a sudden surge of intense and inexplicable emotion; when a compelling dream wakes you; when a vivid memory wells up within you; when something you say or do causes you to wonder, 'Where did that come from?' It is appealing to think that you can get by without paying a lot of attention to what's going on down there in the unconscious, but it is impossible to live exclusively on the surface. When you try to focus solely on the day-to-day, conflicts and problems often rise up from below demanding your attention: you get depressed and can't understand why; you feel powerless to end an addiction; you develop a seemingly irrational fear.

You might think of the unconscious as your mermaid tail. When it flexes its muscles below the surface, it gives a powerful thrust to your life and provides vital energy for everything you say and do.

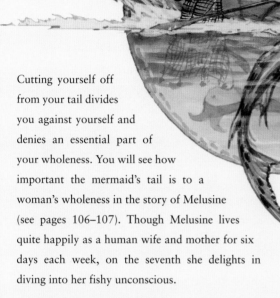

Cutting yourself off from your tail divides you against yourself and denies an essential part of your wholeness. You will see how important the mermaid's tail is to a woman's wholeness in the story of Melusine (see pages 106–107). Though Melusine lives quite happily as a human wife and mother for six days each week, on the seventh she delights in diving into her fishy unconscious.

Tap into your Unconscious

Engaging in inner work can be a similar retreat from the ordinary for you. Setting aside time each day or each week for journaling, active imagination exercises, meditation, creative projects, rituals or dreamwork might feel strange at first, like learning to breathe underwater. But the rewards are rich, and it's lots of fun as well.

Inner work can make you more self-assured and independent. It puts you in touch with your intuition and gives your wild side time to play. It teaches you to understand the language of story and symbol through which the unconscious communicates in dreams and imagination. It connects you to an ever-bubbling source of strength, personal growth and renewal.

Best of all, after diving deep, you can always surface and return to your familiar surroundings. Like Aymee, whose encounter with the mermaid filled her nets with a bounty of fish to nourish her village through the Arctic winter, you come home after your inner work brimming with insights and practical resources for everyday living.

Your own True Face

The most fruitful way to think about the characters and situations you encounter in dreams and other kinds of inner work is as hidden aspects of yourself. Though the images in your dreams may seem weird and confusing, when worked with patiently, they yield insights into your personality and helpful guidance for meeting the challenges and conflicts that your life presents.

✳ ✳ ✳

Exploring the meaning of a dream is like catching a glimpse of your reflection in the water. What you see may at first seem distorted or strange, but when you look carefully you recognize that it is your own true face.

Before she finds the mermaid entangled in her fishing net, Aymee meets her in a dream. In the dream world Aymee herself is the mermaid – an angry goddess of the sea like Sedna (see page 100), whose severed fingers became the creatures of the deep in Inuit mythology. Myths and dreams are similar in that both draw power from their

ability to transform the invisible forces of the unconscious mind into images that human beings can perceive and relate to. In the dream Aymee's resolve to find food for her people is symbolized by her own body transforming into a bounty of fish – sufficient that no one in her village need go hungry.

When Aymee meets the mermaid again in the waking world, she is able to act bravely because she perceives the mermaid as a soul sister, whose long dark hair and female body mirror Aymee's own.

Having recognized the mermaid as a reflection of herself, Aymee is patient

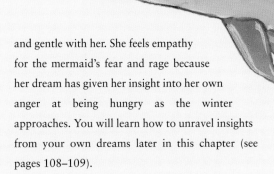

and gentle with her. She feels empathy for the mermaid's fear and rage because her dream has given her insight into her own anger at being hungry as the winter approaches. You will learn how to unravel insights from your own dreams later in this chapter (see pages 108–109).

Tap into the Collective Imagination

In addition to working with dreams and with images found in mermaid tales and other myths, there is a third great channel that you can use to delve into the unconscious part of your mind. That channel is the imagination. As Carl Jung pointed out, the images that arise in dreams and occur in myths often correspond exactly to the images that appear in the creative imagination of painters, poets and writers.

In Jung's view, artistic images do not need to be passed from person to person by culture or migration. Images of the mermaid, to take one example, have arisen spontaneously all over the world and throughout time because their source is the collective imagination of the human race. Though the details differ, mermaid stories, dreams and art evoke similar feelings and raise similar issues wherever they appear because they are part of the human heritage, part of what makes us human.

But you don't need to be an artist or a poet to explore the imagination. The technique of active imagination that you will learn later in this chapter (see pages 110–111) requires only that you are assertive enough to set aside a room and a block of time for yourself. As you will discover in the story of Melusine that follows (see pages 106–107), to do inner work a woman needs time alone and enough freedom, privacy and security to journey into her inner world.

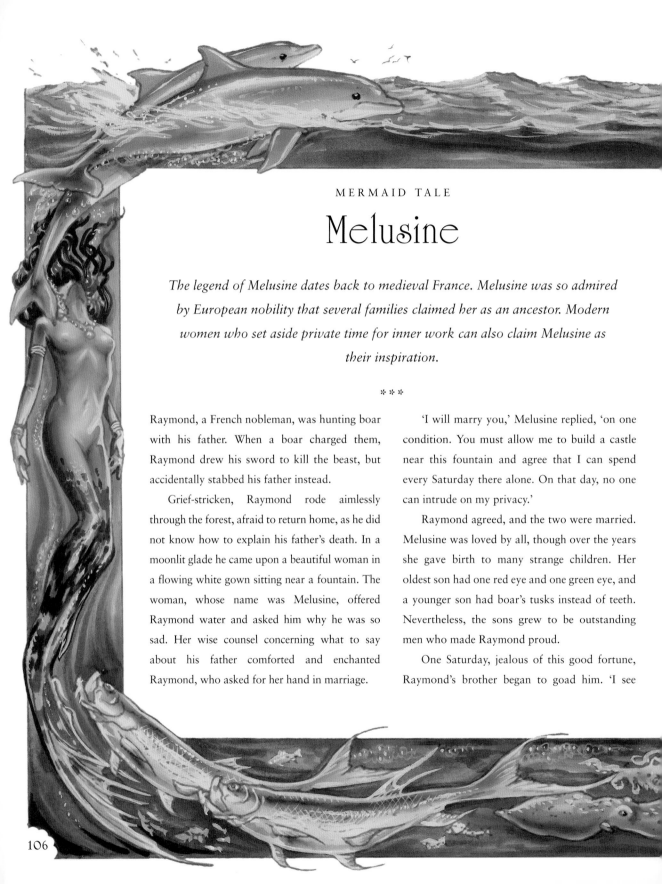

Melusine

The legend of Melusine dates back to medieval France. Melusine was so admired by European nobility that several families claimed her as an ancestor. Modern women who set aside private time for inner work can also claim Melusine as their inspiration.

* * *

Raymond, a French nobleman, was hunting boar with his father. When a boar charged them, Raymond drew his sword to kill the beast, but accidentally stabbed his father instead.

Grief-stricken, Raymond rode aimlessly through the forest, afraid to return home, as he did not know how to explain his father's death. In a moonlit glade he came upon a beautiful woman in a flowing white gown sitting near a fountain. The woman, whose name was Melusine, offered Raymond water and asked him why he was so sad. Her wise counsel concerning what to say about his father comforted and enchanted Raymond, who asked for her hand in marriage.

'I will marry you,' Melusine replied, 'on one condition. You must allow me to build a castle near this fountain and agree that I can spend every Saturday there alone. On that day, no one can intrude on my privacy.'

Raymond agreed, and the two were married. Melusine was loved by all, though over the years she gave birth to many strange children. Her oldest son had one red eye and one green eye, and a younger son had boar's tusks instead of teeth. Nevertheless, the sons grew to be outstanding men who made Raymond proud.

One Saturday, jealous of this good fortune, Raymond's brother began to goad him. 'I see

your wife is away again today,' he taunted. 'You can't deny that your sons look strange. You must have heard the rumours. Some say a demon lover visits Melusine's castle each Saturday. Others say that she is a witch who summons her coven on Saturday night. You must watch closely and find out exactly what she does.'

Though he tried, Raymond could not banish these suspicious imaginings. One Saturday he climbed onto a balcony of Melusine's castle and peered through a keyhole into her dressing room. There he saw his lovely wife laughing and splashing in a large bath – the lower half of her body transformed into the scales and tail of a huge fish!

Raymond tried very hard to conceal his horror. But when one of his sons died at the hands of another and Melusine tried to comfort him, he thrust her away, saying, 'Get out of my sight, you hateful serpent.'

White with shock and despair, Melusine cried, 'Oh, my love, you have betrayed me. Now I must leave you for ever.'

Raymond wept an apology, but the damage was done. Melusine ran from the castle, never to be seen again, though late that night a nursemaid saw a figure in white bend tenderly over the cradle of the youngest child and slip away. As she fled, the nurse could clearly see a fishtail peeking from beneath her gown.

Dreamwork

Dreams take you underwater – beneath the busy surface where currents of insight and understanding flow. The best time to start dreamwork is as soon as you've reached waking consciousness. Keep a notebook and pen near your bed, and write down whatever you remember as soon as you awaken. Recording your dreams has a remarkable effect. Words catch hold of elusive dream images and draw them up to consciousness where you can see them more clearly. Once you have recorded the details of your dreams, work more deeply with your notes when you have the time. Like Melusine, you may wish to set aside a few hours on Saturday to dive into your dream notebook and explore the meaning of the images that you've caught.

* * *

HERE'S WHAT TO DO

1 **Make associations.** Dreams do not waste your time. Assume that every person, place, colour, sound, situation and event in your dream has swum into consciousness to tell you something. Go through your dream and write down every association you can for each image. An association is any feeling, word, memory or idea that pops up in response to an image.

For instance, say you dream that you are in a summer garden. For associations with 'summer garden' you could list: lying on green grass, flower beds, weeds, my grandmother's roses, apple tree, Garden of Eden … Do the same for each person, place, colour, sound, situation and event in your dream.

2 **Make personal connections.** Look over your list of associations for each image and decide which associations 'click' – that is, which spontaneously evoke a lot of energy or strong feeling. For each association that clicks, ask yourself: what part of me is that? What do I have in common with that? Where have I seen it in my life? Make notes about what you discover.

For example, say you have a strong emotional response to 'my grandmother's roses'. Thinking back, you remember that the roses were so beautiful because your grandmother spent many hours every week weeding, fertilizing and pruning. This connection reminds you of the frustration you have felt lately because of having insufficient time to spend on things you care about.

3 **Find the message.** The last step in the process is to draw the associations and connections together into a unified picture. Read over your notes and ask yourself: what important message is this dream trying to communicate? What changes is it advising me to make in my life?

The message you might find is that you care about how you look and need to spend more time on 'personal gardening' – activities that make you feel as beautiful as your grandmother's roses. The dream seems to be advising you to get a great haircut, sign up for an exercise class, have a massage, eat salads for lunch.

Don't expect your dream messages to be totally clear immediately. You will know you are on the right track when an interpretation points the way out of a stuck place or gives you a sudden surge of new life energy. Like Aymee untangling the strands of the mermaid's hair from her net, you need to be gentle and patient, but the time you spend on dreamwork will be amply rewarded.

Active Imagination

Active imagination is a dialogue between you and parts of yourself that live in the unconscious. It is similar to dreaming, except that you are fully awake. Your conscious participation in the process distinguishes active imagination from daydreaming and other less useful kinds of fantasy. Just as in dreams, the characters and events with which you converse in active imagination are images that have arisen from the unconscious part of your own mind. Even though you may feel that you are 'making it up', any image that arises in your imagination comes from you and can thus help you get in touch with inner parts of yourself. Active imagination is an especially good way to access your feelings. For this exercise you may need a notebook or journal.

* * *

HERE'S WHAT TO DO

1 **Set aside a place and time** where you can be completely private and undisturbed. Though it's essential to be alone during the process, if you are concerned that you might be overwhelmed by what you experience, make sure there is someone available for you to go to or call, though this is seldom necessary.

2 **Decide how to record your dialogue.** Some people like to write out their dialogue in a notebook or journal, indicating who is speaking, as in a play script. Others prefer to type it out on a computer.

3 **Sit comfortably,** close your eyes and take several deep breaths, focusing your attention on the rise and fall of your abdomen as you breathe.

4 **Invite an image to arise** in your mind, once you feel centred and relaxed. If, after a period of waiting, nothing comes, try travelling in your mind to a place that has particular meaning for you and see who shows up. For instance, you might imagine that you are walking along a deserted beach. Alternatively, ask a mood you have been experiencing to take the form of an image so that you can understand it better; for example, ask, 'Who is the one inside me who is angry today? Please take some form so that I can speak to you.'

5 **When an image appears,** do not judge or reject it. Assume that it has something important to say to you. To get the dialogue going, ask a question such as: 'Who are you?', 'What do you want?' or 'What do you have to say?' Write down your question and then, without editing or censoring, write down what the image says or does in response. Note down also any feelings you have during the dialogue and any that you perceive as being felt by the image.

6 **Continue the conversation,** sticking with the image that you started with and letting your imagination flow, until you feel that you have arrived at some kind of resolution. Sometimes your active-imagination dialogue may continue over several sessions before you feel that you have learned everything you can.

7 **Keep in mind** that – although it's important that you do not consciously control or manipulate the conversation – you always have the right to argue back or say no, and to refuse to go along with the suggestion that you act in any way that is harmful or contrary to your highest values.

DIVING AND SURFACING

CHAPTER 8
LADY OF THE WATERS

* * *

Sabrina fair

Listen where thou art sitting

Under the glassy, cool, translucent wave,

In twisted braids of lilies knitting

The loose train of thy amber-dropping hair;

Listen for dear honour's sake,

Goddess of the silver lake,

Listen and save.

JOHN MILTON (1608–1674), 'SABRINA FAIR'

Mermaids can be a source of profound spiritual gifts. From earliest times they have been associated with the Divine Feminine – God in female form. As the sea goddesses of the ancient world, as Christian saints and angels and as wise women and spiritual teachers in every age, mermaids have been called upon (just as they are called upon by the speaker in Milton's song) to listen, heal and save.

What are the links between the mermaid and spiritual faith? And how can you reach out to the mermaid as sea goddess and saint, or as an empowering aspect of the human imagination and spirit, and discover a powerful source of healing and inspiration?

This chapter explores the stories of the mermaid associated with Zennor, in Cornwall, whose image carved into a bench end in a parish church inspired the wonderful novel *The Mermaid Chair* by Sue Monk Kidd. As you will discover, the mermaid has strong links with the feminine face of God: with the Virgin Mary and Mary Magdalene and with a tradition of the mermaid as a miracle worker, saint and healer. Mermaid rituals and meditations invite you to reach out to the mermaid as a representative of the Divine Feminine for healing and spiritual wisdom.

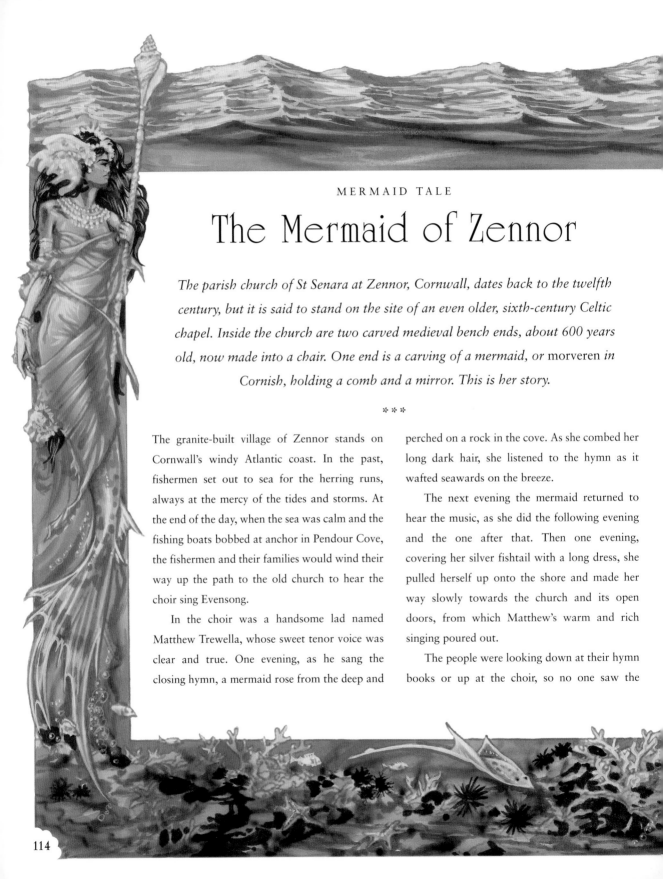

The Mermaid of Zennor

The parish church of St Senara at Zennor, Cornwall, dates back to the twelfth century, but it is said to stand on the site of an even older, sixth-century Celtic chapel. Inside the church are two carved medieval bench ends, about 600 years old, now made into a chair. One end is a carving of a mermaid, or morveren *in Cornish, holding a comb and a mirror. This is her story.*

* * *

The granite-built village of Zennor stands on Cornwall's windy Atlantic coast. In the past, fishermen set out to sea for the herring runs, always at the mercy of the tides and storms. At the end of the day, when the sea was calm and the fishing boats bobbed at anchor in Pendour Cove, the fishermen and their families would wind their way up the path to the old church to hear the choir sing Evensong.

In the choir was a handsome lad named Matthew Trewella, whose sweet tenor voice was clear and true. One evening, as he sang the closing hymn, a mermaid rose from the deep and perched on a rock in the cove. As she combed her long dark hair, she listened to the hymn as it wafted seawards on the breeze.

The next evening the mermaid returned to hear the music, as she did the following evening and the one after that. Then one evening, covering her silver fishtail with a long dress, she pulled herself up onto the shore and made her way slowly towards the church and its open doors, from which Matthew's warm and rich singing poured out.

The people were looking down at their hymn books or up at the choir, so no one saw the

morveren as she stood in the shadows at the church door, drinking in Matthew's dark eyes and sweet voice. Every evening after that, the *morveren* put on her long dress and came to church to listen and look. She heard the silent prayers of women whose husbands and sons sailed at the mercy of the wind and storms. She saw young lovers exchange glances over the top of their hymn books. But before the last note faded, she slipped away to catch the tide.

One night, as Matthew and the choir sang, the *morveren*'s eyes were drawn to the light of the moon shining through a narrow window on the south wall of the chancel. Seeing the saintly figure depicted there in coloured glass, the *morveren* caught her breath with a sigh.

At that moment Matthew stopped singing, and his eyes met hers. In that instant he loved her. Though the *morveren* quickly withdrew, Matthew ran down the aisle of the church and out of the door after her.

'Wait,' he cried, 'I will go with you', for he had seen the fishtail peeking from beneath her gown. Catching up the mermaid into his arms, he ran with her to the ocean's edge and plunged with her into the waves.

Never again were Matthew and the *morveren* seen in church or anywhere in Zennor. But the fishermen hear him still, singing love songs to his mermaid bride deep under the sea.

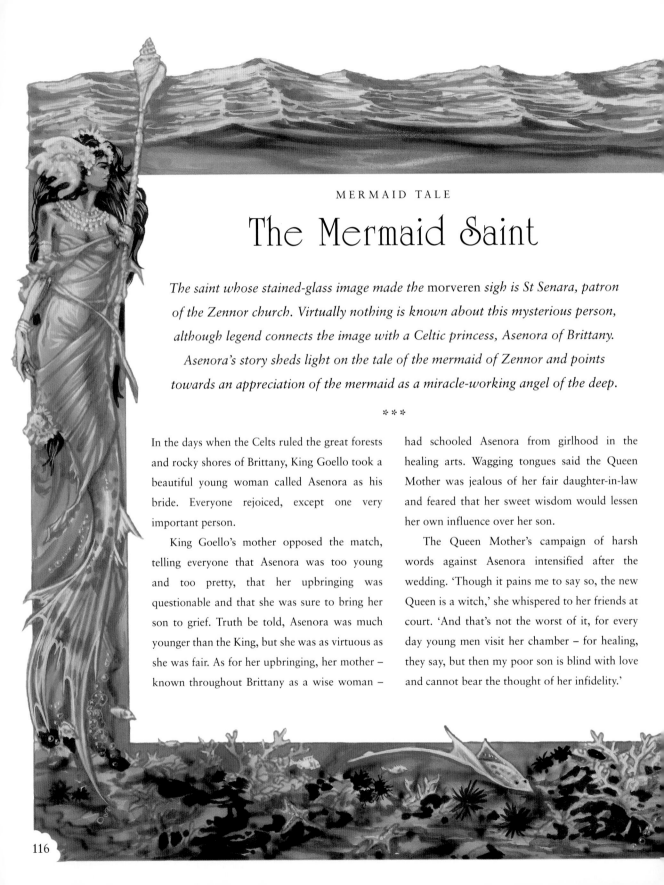

The Mermaid Saint

The saint whose stained-glass image made the morveren *sigh is St Senara, patron of the Zennor church. Virtually nothing is known about this mysterious person, although legend connects the image with a Celtic princess, Asenora of Brittany. Asenora's story sheds light on the tale of the mermaid of Zennor and points towards an appreciation of the mermaid as a miracle-working angel of the deep.*

***

In the days when the Celts ruled the great forests and rocky shores of Brittany, King Goello took a beautiful young woman called Asenora as his bride. Everyone rejoiced, except one very important person.

King Goello's mother opposed the match, telling everyone that Asenora was too young and too pretty, that her upbringing was questionable and that she was sure to bring her son to grief. Truth be told, Asenora was much younger than the King, but she was as virtuous as she was fair. As for her upbringing, her mother – known throughout Brittany as a wise woman –

had schooled Asenora from girlhood in the healing arts. Wagging tongues said the Queen Mother was jealous of her fair daughter-in-law and feared that her sweet wisdom would lessen her own influence over her son.

The Queen Mother's campaign of harsh words against Asenora intensified after the wedding. 'Though it pains me to say so, the new Queen is a witch,' she whispered to her friends at court. 'And that's not the worst of it, for every day young men visit her chamber – for healing, they say, but then my poor son is blind with love and cannot bear the thought of her infidelity.'

On a day when Goello was away on a hunt, the Queen Mother struck. She ordered soldiers loyal to her to arrest a young knight as he left the Queen's apartment. Though he protested that the Queen had but dressed his wounded shoulder, the knight was hustled away and the Queen herself was seized, accused of infidelity and condemned to be burned.

'Put me to the fire if you will,' Asenora said bravely as soldiers lashed her to the stake, 'but know that you burn as well Goello's heir.'

At these words, the unhappy rumblings among the soldiers increased greatly. Fearful of King Goello's wrath, should it be known that they had murdered his unborn child, they refused to light the fire.

'So be it,' the Queen Mother declared. 'Let the sea decide her guilt or innocence.' And so, at the Queen Mother's direction, Asenora was placed in a barrel, which was nailed shut and thrown into the sea.

What happened after the barrel floated out of sight cannot be known for certain, but some months later a young woman holding a baby to her breast was washed up on the Irish coast. The child was called Budoc – 'the drowned one'. Years later, when he and his mother sailed back to Brittany, they stopped for provisions at Cornwall and founded the parishes of Zennor (Sinar) and Budoc.

All Asenora would say of her ordeal was that an angel with long, dark hair fed her, attended her childbed beneath the waves and made sure that she and her son came safely to land.

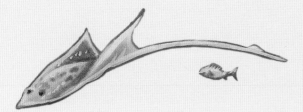

Our Lady of the Waters

It is tempting to speculate that the Cornish morveren *who married chorister Matthew Trewella beneath the sea is the same mermaid angel who tended Asenora and her unborn child. This identification would explain why the* morveren *was drawn to visit Zennor in the first place and why the image of St Senara would make her sigh.*

* * *

Intriguing as these speculations are, more wonderful still is the rich tradition of the mermaid as miracle worker, saint and healer that lies behind both stories. This thread of the mermaid myth winds through many of the mermaid ideas you have explored – the sea goddesses of the ancient world, the denigration of the siren as a temptress by the Church, and the tradition of the mermaid as teacher and wise woman. It also leads to a fascinating link between the mermaid and the biblical Maries: both the Virgin Mary and Mary Magdalene.

As you have read, the Great Mother goddesses of the ancient world came from the sea. Among these was Astarte, the Phoenician goddess in whose temple Atargatis, the first mermaid, served. Many historians have speculated that Phoenician sailors traded as far away as Cornwall, from where they brought back tin to make bronze. Among the divinities that these early mariners would have carried with them to Cornwall was the mermaid goddess. Coins have been excavated at early Phoenician sites imprinted with the image of a mermaid, and it is not hard to imagine Phoenician sailors telling mermaid tales to their Cornish trading partners.

The beliefs of the Phoenician and, later, the Roman merchant sailors who visited Cornwall to trade for tin had important similarities with the beliefs of the pagan Celts who were Cornwall's original inhabitants. In all three cultures, water was

connected to the feminine and to healing. Wells and springs often became sacred shrines, where votive offerings for healing, for children or for a fruitful harvest were left for the divinity said to live in the waters. Cornwall has many of these sacred wells, where today people still leave offerings in the old way. As you have read, in cultures all over the world, wells and springs are the natural domains of the mermaid.

The Merging of Folk Belief and Christianity

When Christianity came to Cornwall around 600 CE, it is thought that many of the original Celtic inhabitants fled, taking their stories and beliefs with them. Some settled in Brittany, which further helps to explain the link between Asenora and the mermaid of Zennor. In its drive to Christianize Cornwall over the next several centuries, the Roman Church converted the old places and the old stories to its use. Pagan wells became holy wells and were renamed for saints, and

Christian churches were built on Celtic sacred sites. Thus it makes perfect sense that the twelfth-century Zennor church was built over a sixth-century Celtic chapel; that Asenora, the Celtic princess, would became St Senara; and that in the later Christian-era story, the mermaid of Zennor would come regularly to Evensong before seducing and marrying a member of the choir, in a tale that is reminiscent of the temptress sirens of old.

It is also no surprise that local legend holds that a sacred spring on a moor near Zennor is a spot where children used to be taken for healing, and that a cross on top of the south porch of Zennor church is said to have magical healing powers. In Zennor, it seems, as has happened all over the world, folk beliefs have merged with the Christian faith and the mermaid goddess has become a Christian angel and healing saint.

The Mermaid and the Feminine Face of God

But there is another fascinating connection between the mermaid and Christianity. In churches all over the world, especially near the Mediterranean, the

Virgin Mary is venerated with rites and fervour reminiscent of the worship of the Great Mother goddesses of old. The Virgin's link with the goddess tradition – and with the mermaid – is reflected in her name. Mary, or Maria, comes from the Latin *mare*, which means 'sea'.

As befits the son of a sea goddess, Mary's son, Jesus, is called a 'fisher of men'. British folk legend holds that Jesus accompanied his maternal uncle Joseph of Arimathea, a tin merchant, on a trading trip to Cornwall and other places in England, where he is said to have conferred with Celtic Druids about their ancient beliefs. Like his mother Mary, Jesus has a mermaid connection. His dual nature as both God and man is compared in some medieval texts to the mermaid, who is, at the same time, both a woman and a fish.

But it is the other Mary – Mary Magdalene – whose story ties in most closely with the mermaid. *The Golden Legend*, a medieval book of saints' lives written between 1260 and 1275, says that some years after the Resurrection, three women named Mary – Mary Magdalene, Mary-Salome, the mother of John the Apostle, and Mary-Jacob, the wife of Cleophas – fled into exile in France. They arrived at Saintes-Maries-de-la-Mer (Three Maries of the Sea) bringing with them, some versions of the story say, the heir of Jesus born of his union with Mary Magdalene: the 'royal bloodline' that may be the *sangraal*, or Holy Grail.

Here the story returns to the mermaid, for the line of French kings said to be the guardians of the Grail are the Merovingians – *mer*, of course, signifying both Mary and the sea. Medieval coats of arms often depict the fleur-de-lis emblem of the Merovingians surrounded by sirens, and legend says that an ancestress of the Merovingians was a mermaid!

Whatever you choose to believe, it seems clear that the mermaid – goddess and angel, siren temptress and saint, healer and miracle worker – is a more profound spiritual symbol than popular culture has given her credit for. The deeper you delve into mermaid lore – and into your own mind and spirit with the mermaid as your guide – the more certain you will be that the mermaid is rising to the surface of culture and consciousness in our time, to claim her rightful place within the tradition of feminine sacred wisdom.

Water Rituals

Whatever your current spiritual beliefs, the practices described here and overleaf can help you deepen your connection to the most sacred part of yourself.

Water has always been used in rituals, from Christian baptism to bathing in holy rivers like the Ganges. It's easy to create your own mermaid water rituals, but here are a few ideas to get you started.

* * *

HERE'S WHAT TO DO

- **Water and salt purification.** Moisten a cup of Dead Sea salt or coarse kosher salt with a few tablespoons of water. Begin to fill a bath with warm water. Stand in the bath as it fills, pick up a handful of salt paste and use it as a scrub on your arms, elbows, legs, shoulders and feet. Avoid your face and any sensitive tissues, because salt can burn. As you scrub away the dead skin, consider what else you wish to wash away: fear, grief, shame, anger. Sink down into the warm water and let everything you wish to release dissolve into it.

- **Sea wishes.** If you live near the coast or visit the seaside, find some time alone to send a wish into the domain of the mermaid goddess. Sit comfortably at the tide line and use your finger or a stick to draw or write in the sand a wish or intention for your future. Know that as the tide comes in, your wish will be carried into the ocean of future possibilities.

- **Scrying.** Gazing into a bowl of water is a time-honoured way of connecting with your inner knowing. Fill a shallow dish with water and place it so that you can look into it from an angle. Relax your body and allow your gaze to be soft and unfocused. If you have a particular question, voice it out loud and see what appears, or simply invite images to arise on the surface of the water.

Mermaid Pilgrimages

Visiting places connected with the mermaid in her various forms can be a wonderful way to further your spiritual understanding. Be sure to read up on the places you visit and to seek out local guidebooks and information. Plan to spend enough time at a site to absorb its atmosphere. Take along your journal and write about what you observe and how the place makes you feel. Though the list of mermaid-related places around the world is lengthy, here are some ideas to inspire you.

* * *

HERE'S WHAT TO DO

- **Churches.** Many medieval and Romanesque churches have mermaid carvings, including Sherborne Abbey, Dorset; Ripon Minster, Yorkshire; and St Peter's, Bologna, Italy.

- **Holy wells.** Wells and springs said to have healing waters are found throughout the British Isles and Europe, including Mabon Holy Well, Cornwall; St Winifrid's Well, Holywell, Wales; St Brigid's Well, Liscannor, County Clare, Ireland; and Lourdes, France.

- **Ruins.** Archaeological sites, especially near the Mediterranean, are often connected to the sea goddess in one of her forms; Crete, Malta and Cyprus all have especially potent sea-goddess sites.

- **Galleries with mermaid art.** Spend time with mermaid paintings in any fine art museum you visit, and be sure to see the mermaid statues, should you travel to Copenhagen, Denmark, or Napier, New Zealand.

Mermaid Meditations

Meditating on the Divine Feminine in her mermaid form or as any other goddess, saint or angel helps you to access and honour feminine wisdom in yourself and others. Meditation is not only sitting with your eyes closed. It also includes activities that deepen your awareness.

* * *

HERE'S WHAT TO DO

• **Create a shrine.** Making a sacred space for meditation helps you to connect with forces beyond your everyday life. A meditation shrine does not need to be elaborate, and it can change with your mood or with the seasons. A bookshelf or dresser top covered with a beautiful cloth or scarf makes a fine altar. Decorate your shrine with pictures or small statues of any representations of the Divine Feminine that appeal to you. Add flowers, fruit or other offerings. For a shrine that honours the mermaid, include shells, stones that have been smoothed by the sea, and a bowl of water, perhaps with a flower floating on the surface.

• **Make a personal tidebook.** Connecting with the cycles of nature, such as the tides, can act as a form of meditation. If you live near the coast, purchase a local tide table or download one from the Internet. Track the cycle of high and low tides by checking the tide table each morning. In the evening write in your journal about how your moods or the events of your day mirrored the ebb and flow of the day's tides. Even if you live inland, you can create a personal tidebook by charting your emotional highs and lows for a week. Then add photographs, cuttings from magazines, drawings, poems and journal entries that express what the cycles of high and low tide mean in your life.

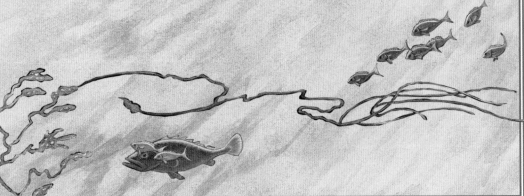

Mermaid Visualization

Visualizing a mermaid and asking her for a personal message is a good way to communicate with the wisest part of yourself.

* * *

HERE'S WHAT TO DO

1 **Sit comfortably,** close your eyes and take several deep breaths, focusing your attention on the rise and fall of your abdomen as you breathe, until you feel centred and relaxed.

2 **Allow the image to arise** in your mind of a place that might be the domain of a mermaid, such as a rocky beach or seashore, a fountain or well in a forest clearing, or a peaceful and secluded lake. It can be a real place that you have visited or somewhere that you imagine.

3 **Take some time to visualize** the place clearly by noting details that appeal to each of your senses. If you are on a beach, hear the splash of the waves; if you are in a forest, smell the leaves and earth.

4 **Now imagine a mermaid** in this scene, in any form that appeals to you. She could be a woman in a long dress standing near a fountain, or a fishtailed siren sitting on a seaside rock combing her hair.

5 **Tell the mermaid** that you have come to honour her as a representative of the Divine Feminine. Ask her to teach you something that will help you access and appreciate your own feminine wisdom. Then wait for her answer, which may come in the form of words, images or feelings.

6 **Thank the mermaid,** once her message seems complete, and take as long as you need to return to ordinary consciousness.

7 **Write about the message** in your journal so that it can continue to unfold.

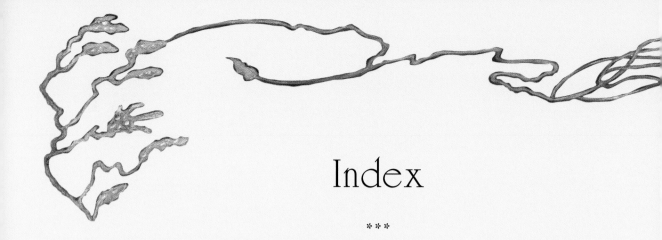

Index

* * *

Acknowledgements

* * *

Sue Monk Kidd's wonderful novel *The Mermaid Chair* inspired me to look more deeply into myths about the mermaid. Two excellent collections of mermaid stories, *Mermaid Tales from Around the World* by Mary Pope Osborne and *A Treasury of Mermaids* by Shirley Climo, guided me to stories to explore, adapt and retell. *Mermaids* by Beatrice Phillpotts provided essential background. The work of Anne Baring and Jules Cashford, Robert Graves, Buffie Johnson, Patience Gent and Scarlett deMason helped me understand the connections between the mermaid and the Goddess. Margaret Starbird and George Pritchard guided my understanding of the mermaid's links to Christianity and the Divine Feminine. *Slaying the Mermaid: Women and the Culture of Sacrifice* by Stephanie Golden provided insights into the psychology of the Little Mermaid. *Inner Work* by Robert A. Johnson grounded my dreamwork and active imagination exercises. *Mermaids: Sirens of the Sea* by Kerry Colburn and *Mermaids* by Elizabeth Ratisseau inspired me with beautifully reproduced mermaid art and well-chosen quotations. To all these and to everyone who has written about the mermaid, my deepest thanks.

Executive Editor Sandra Rigby
Managing Editor Clare Churly
Executive Art Editor Sally Bond
Designers Claire Oldman & Annika Skoog for Cobalt Id
Illustrator David Bergen, Jon Goode
Production Controller Simone Nauerth